MEMENTO

EMBRACING THE DARKNESS

DENNIS (DIZZY) DOAN

EIGHT HORSES
PUBLISHING

Cover Design by Nuno Moreira

Edited by Dr. Jade T. Hidle

I wholeheartedly dedicate this book to my beloved grandparents, who self-lessly nurtured and guided me throughout the beginning of my life, without ever seeking recognition, compensation, or any form of repayment whatsoever. Their mere existence and authenticity taught me the profound beauty of appreciating even life's simplest moments. They exemplified that true worth and personal growth transcend societal labels, prevail-ing against any obstacles that life may throw one's way. Their support and reassurance throughout my childhood instilled in me a sense of hope, reminding me that there is always a reason to persevere and face life's challenges head-on.

I also extend this dedication to all those who find themselves lost, yearning to be discovered. It is crucial to acknowledge that feeling adrift and devoid of hope is a natural part of life. It is perfectly normal to be uncertain about what lies ahead in the future. Based on my experiences in life thus far, I can firmly assure you that your "moment" doesn't always come when YOU'RE ready for it, and there may be times that it will come when you're NOT ready. But that defining moment when everything does align is the moment you can unequivocally know it's truly meant to be. And that in itself is worth waiting and fighting for.

Last but certainly not least, this is dedicated to those who doubted me, those who believed I would never achieve anything and thought my path would lead to nowhere. It is for those who dismissed my dreams, convinced that following my passion would never take me anywhere. This message is also to those who chose to discourage rather than uplift those in need, using their words to belittle others instead of offering a helping hand. It is to those individuals who used their influence to dampen the potential of others, instead of using it to inspire and empower. You, in fact, fueled the very fire that was hidden beneath the brush of my life. Without your skepticism, I would have remained complacent with mediocrity and the illusion of victory.

CONTENTS

PREFACE

For those who are already familiar with my story, you know that *art* has been my medium for connecting with the world throughout my whole life. You may be unaware that I had been expressing myself through words long before I acquired the skills to vividly portray my innermost thoughts on a human canvas. Painting my true essence with needles came later, but my journey as a wordsmith began much earlier.

Now, more than ever, I believe it is crucial for me to document the profound significance of my past—the triumphs that have shaped my journey thus far—so that I may fully grasp and appreciate the beauty that exists within both the shadows and the light that it casts on my life. When you actively and passionately strive for personal growth each and every day, your efforts often go unnoticed by *yourself* as the person living the moment. And the goals that you *do* manage to achieve often become overshadowed by the moments of failure and darkness in between. I have been my own harshest critic, far more demanding and punishing of myself than anyone else could *EVER* be.

My life was neither the most tragic nor the most privileged; I did not endure abject poverty *nor* did I revel in luxury as a child. Although my story may be unfamiliar to you, it is a narrative shared by many children who grew up in neighborhoods like the one I grew up in. Throughout this journey of self-discovery, I have encountered countless trials and tribulations, learning not only to *adapt* to and *embrace* failure, but train my mind to *absorb* these setbacks as invaluable lessons rather than mere misfortunes. I have come to appreciate these mistakes and become grateful that they arose early in my life, callusing my heart, body, and mind for the greater challenges that lie ahead.

It is all too familiar for the world to simply write off others' achievements or pursuits of fame and fortune. People often try to shield themselves from the potential blow to their egos and lack of ambition by attributing such successes to mere luck or labeling it as an outcome of "ideal" or "privileged" circumstances. Consequently, this assumption blinds them and they fail to recognize that becoming a so-called "overnight sensation" is a process that typically spans years, if not decades. These pessimistic individuals, often driven by jealousy and hostility, spend a significant portion of their time attempting to discredit those capable of accomplishing such remarkable feats. It is crucial to resist this toxic mindset, as it can serve as the seed that blossoms into self-destruction and ultimately leads you to an acceptance of mediocrity for your own life. Guard yourself against falling into this toxic rhythm at all costs.

No matter how you measure it, success is more the result of conscious action and unrivaled determination than random chance. The concept of "overnight success" is an illusion. That one night of achievement is the culmination of years of trial and error spent cultivating and forging the knowledge and abilities necessary to bring it about. If you put in the effort, you will inevitably be rewarded. Someone once said, "Give your life to your work, and your work will give you a life." Anyone who solely fixates on reaching only significant milestones overlooks the profound truth that it is the accumulation of *progress made over time* that ultimately forms an insurmountable whole.

It's tempting to blame external factors such as our environment, authorities, or life circumstances for our shortcomings in regards to our successes or lack thereof. But this is a pointless endeavor. While our initial social and economic positions may differ, our potential achievements are ultimately determined by our level of conviction. At our core, *we are all human beings.* In my opinion, those who have endured unimaginable hardships possess an undeniable advantage over those who are granted every advantage from birth. As survivors, we do not have the luxury of having the tools of life *handed* to us; instead, we must *create* our own. Though there will undoubtedly be challenges, missteps, and disappointments along the way, these experiences will equip us to protect ourselves as we forge ahead in a way that no amount of money or privilege can.

Writing this book is an opportunity for me to heal the wounds I have suffered, including those I inflicted upon myself physically and psychologically. Symbiotically, this book will aid both the reader and me in our healing journeys. It is my honor to have all of you join me in reliving this transformative journey and gaining the understanding and illumination needed to avoid similar pitfalls.

There is no need to be ashamed about making mistakes because they are an integral component of the learning process. The alternative of not trying at all can bring about feelings of shame and lifelong regret. My sincere hope for today's youth is that they will find refuge in knowing that they are not alone as they navigate the turbulent path to adulthood. I know firsthand how torturous it can be to be forced to contend with your own image in the mirror and the self-doubt that runs through your head constantly. But rest assured, the light at the end of the tunnel actually becomes more visible the further one travels into the darkness of life's difficulties, contrary to popular belief. Never discount the importance of this simple fact. I, too, have been overcome by the shadows at one time or another. But the remnants of even the tiniest embers were enough to spark a raging wildfire within, and I was able to radiate my own light.

Your spark will come.

INTRODUCTION

It was a long, difficult journey that required a lot of introspection before I could fully analyze, comprehend, and embrace the circumstances that forced me to construct the life that I have now.. In the past, I was consumed by only the present moments, fixated on evading my past, leaving little room to acknowledge and appreciate the beautiful disaster of a future that I was building for myself. It was as if I had been trying so hard to assemble a picture-perfect puzzle, only to discover that its true beauty actually lay in the thousands of imperfect parts that came together to create a masterpiece.

In the depths of my anxiety, I discovered a way to gain a sense of control of my mind and of my life. Rather than succumbing to the darkness, I sought solace in absorbing the positive emotions and optimism of those around me, harnessing their power to fuel my motivation. This was my strategy to evade confronting the harsh truth of my spiritual deterioration as I faced a whirlwind of adversity throughout my childhood. The cards of misfortune that I was dealt had taught me valuable lessons that infused my life with newfound purpose and significance. Though it required constant effort to heal my wounds and prevent them from reopening over and over again, I took comfort in knowing that I, at least, possessed the knowledge and had forged the tools necessary to manage it all through these experiences.

My persistence became my salvation. I made a vow to myself that I would not settle on merely becoming just another statistic from my neighborhood. I refused to let the limitations imposed by my upbringing dictate my aspirations and expectations for myself. The fear of being labeled a "waste of life" propelled me forward, fueling a fierce determination within me. I was adamant in proving to the world and its *circumstances* that the power of such effort and resilience, possessed by individuals just like me who didn't start the race with the same advantages, should never be underestimated. Driven by an unyielding desire to demonstrate that even a poor Asian child born in America, destined for insignificance, had the audacity to believe that he had the ability to change the world. I committed myself to that very endeavor.

IT WASN'T ALWAYS LIKE THIS

Flashes of the shattered glass and porcelain littered all over the kitchen floor, a grim reminder of the chaos that awaited us. I snapped back to reality as I heard the sound of my mom urgently opening the kitchen window, bracing herself for what was coming. It had become an eerie routine—my dad's weekly drunken homecoming, triggering the mayhem that plagued our lives.

I usually had my older brother with me, my anchor in those stormy times, who would take me in his arms, his presence a source of comfort and reassurance. He would whisper words of consolation, promising that everything would eventually be okay. Of course, there were some occasions when he was unable to be there to rescue me. Whenever things took a turn for the worse, my instinct was to find a safe haven. I would run to my room, turning off all of the lights to hide in the darkness, or seek shelter in the bathroom, where I could still hear the deafening symphony of screaming without being seen just in case I needed to step in if things took a turn for the worst.

As I heard the familiar creaking of the emergency brake of my dad's dark gold 1991 Honda Accord sedan pulling into its designated parking spot at College Gardens Apartments, a knot formed in my stomach, twisting with anticipation and dread. I cautiously approached the window as instructed by mom, peering through the curtains, straining to assess the level of dad's drunkenness. If he stumbled out of the car, vomiting and swaying in his plastered state, he was too far gone to provoke an argument or throw his rage at us. On these relieving nights, I would open the front door for him, ensuring he made it inside the apartment without risking a dangerous fall down the concrete stairs leading up to our unit. It was an unspoken agreement, a way to protect him from himself.

But if my dad emerged from the car *without* any signs of blacking out, a surge of panic surged through my veins. Without a second thought, I would run into my mom's bedroom to be next to her, the only place I believed I offered some semblance of safety. We hid together beneath the covers, pretending to sleep, hoping that our stillness and the illusion of slumber would be enough to deter my dad's fury. It was our only defense, a shield against the storm that threatened to tear our family apart.

The weight of our situation pressed heavily on my heart. The fear that loomed in our home were constant reminders of the battles we faced. Yet, within the depths of darkness, a flicker of resilience burned inside me. I yearned for a different future—for a life free from the echoes of broken fragments and the looming presence of fear. Even at the age of four, I held onto that glimmer of hope, knowing that one day, I would break free from this cycle, and create a better story for myself and my family.

It wasn't always like this.

FALL OF SAIGON

F or those who don't know me, I go by Dennis (Dizzy) Doan. I was born on April 26th, 1990 in Saginaw, Michigan. As the first child to be born in the United States to parents who arrived in the country from Vietnam, I *am* the first generation. My older brother was twelve years old when they arrived.

Despite the fact that I was too young to have any personal memories from that time, I cannot deny the fact that the old family photo albums reveal a great deal. When those moments were captured, I looked around at my family and saw unmistakable expressions of optimism on their faces. They exuded a resolute hope for a better future in this strange land that they were now obligated to call home. This hope was accompanied by a sense of determination. It was a fresh start—an opportunity for them to construct entirely new lives from scratch. It was a chance to leave the haunting echoes of the past behind, releasing the shackles of trauma that had accompanied them on their journeys of life up to that point.

My parents' lives were deeply influenced by the backdrop of the Vietnam War. My mom hailed from Saigon, now known as Ho Chi Minh

City, in the southern region of Vietnam. My dad, on the other hand, originated from Da Nang in the central region. Their love story began as a familiar tale of a poor country boy falling in love with a city girl who lived a comfortable life.

Within my mom's family, *Ông Ngoại* and *Bà Ngoại*, my maternal grandparents, held a respectable position within the middle class. My grandfather, a renowned architect, was responsible for designing several significant government structures in the city during that particular time period. They had the luxury of owning a three-story house. Growing up, my mom enjoyed a relatively privileged life that was strongly influenced by French culture and religion, which were still prevalent in Vietnam at the time because of the former French occupation of the country. She attended a French-Vietnamese school and sang for the church, as did most of her nine siblings. They got to experience a normal childhood filled with extracurriculars. Her parents, together, raised all of their children under one roof, fostering an exceptionally close-knit family.

In contrast, my dad's life was marked by unrelenting sorrow and hardship. He, too, was one of ten children, but only four of his younger siblings shared the same father. My dad was the middle child. When the war saw its conclusion and the country was overrun by Ho Chi Minh's forces, the United States withdrew its military support in 1975. As the North Vietnamese military closed in on Da Nang, my dad and his entire family had to make a hasty escape to the south. My dad was abruptly left behind and had to travel on foot to their destination in the south while carrying the heaviest of his family's belongings because the rest of his family had been whisked away by helicopter. The length of this journey, let alone the willpower and physical fortitude required, is beyond my comprehension. During the Vietnam War, my paternal grandma, *Bà Nội*, served as a nurse, a role that carried immense trauma in itself throughout the period of the war. Many women, including herself, had to cope with the loss of their husbands throughout those tragic years all while shouldering the responsibility of raising a large family. Nevertheless, her determination in the face of adversity was unparalleled, making her a cornerstone of our family. She remains, in our eyes, a true hero. Her ability to raise all of her children in the midst of the fog of war was nothing short of remarkable. The challenges she faced were immense, and yet she found a way to not only be a mom but also to save lives as a nurse in the midst of her struggles. It showed how incredibly tough and resilient she was. Despite the chaos and uncertainty surrounding her, she managed to provide love, care, and protection for her children while also extending her compassion to others in need. Her selflessness and determination to make a positive difference in the lives of those around her were truly extraordinary. She was a shining example of the strength of a mother's love. Her life exemplified the power of human will to overcome adversity and leave a lasting impression on the world. I consider myself incredibly fortunate to have been among the last grandchildren she helped raise.

My Dad's biological father and I

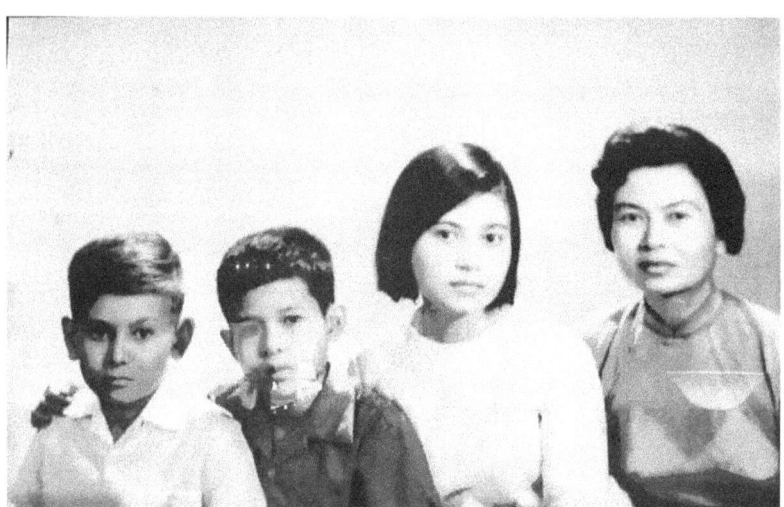

One of Dad's older brothers, Dad ,one of his older sisters, and Grandma

My grandma had many children, but my dad was the only child she had with my own paternal grandpa, Chan Doan. Growing up, my curiosity somehow never led me to question why I had so many grandparents, but as I grew older and put together all of the bits and pieces of information that I had acquired throughout the years, I was able to finally comprehend the dysfunctional dynamics of my family. As a police captain, my grandpa was deeply involved in covert operations to infiltrate the North Vietnamese military, which ultimately led to him spending the majority of his life behind bars. He gave his life to his country, but his ties to his family were the collateral. Consequently, my dad was estranged from his own dad for much of his life. Despite this, he was fortunate to have been raised by his stepdad, whom I grew up believing to be my paternal grandpa (my biological grandpa, however, eventually made his way to the United States).

As a child, the concept of having more than two parents was incredibly mind-blowing to me. I was raised with the belief, instilled in me by my traditional Vietnamese family, that once a man and a woman chose to love each other, their love would endure for a lifetime. The idea of a wedded couple going their separate ways, especially given such a large number of children caught in the midst of it, seemed unfathomable. It was something that I had only witnessed in movies or read about in books.

As I matured, I came to realize that this was a reality many families faced. This realization shattered the innocence and naivety I once held.

Unbeknownst to me at the time, this experience would subconsciously shape my perception of my own family as I journeyed into adulthood. I was unaware of the profound impact it would have on me and how it would manifest in my life.

The understanding that families could undergo such upheaval and fragmentation challenged my preconceived notions of love and stability. It forced me to confront the complexities of human relationships and the fragility of what I had assumed to be unbreakable bonds. It was a lesson that taught me the imperfections and vulnerabilities of the world, but it also opened my eyes to the resilience and adaptability of the human spirit. Through this realization, I began to appreciate the intricacies of family dynamics and the diverse ways in which individuals navigate through life's unpredictable challenges. I recognize that this early revelation played a significant role in shaping my perspectives and attitudes toward family, relationships, and the ever-evolving nature of love. While it initially shattered my childlike beliefs, it ultimately helped me develop a broader and more compassionate understanding. I was more willing to accept the idea of blended families and aware of the fact that there was more than one perspective of the perfect family.

COLLATERAL DAMAGE

The story of my family's lives in Saigon, post-war, was far from a fairy tale. Even today, the consequences of the battles linger, affecting the lives of countless individuals around the world. My dad and his siblings, like many Vietnamese countrymen, surrendered to alcoholism as a means of coping with their misery. They were left impoverished, famished, and emotionally defeated, their once-impenetrable sense of pride and dignity shattered. This pervasive darkness cast a shadow over the entire nation, leaving lasting scars on its people and the generations that followed.

In true Vietnamese spirit, they learned to make the most out of the circumstances that they were dealt and tried to find peace in the simple joys of life. My older brother, who experienced this period as a child, had no contrasting frame of reference and thus perceived the nation's demeanor as a typical part of life. They adjusted to the sorrow and learned to make the best of a difficult situation. The ability to find contentment amidst adversity is a hallmark of the Vietnamese people. Despite the haunting presence of war, they cherished the small moments and embraced the strength derived from unity and perseverance. This shared experience shaped their collective identity and continues to influence their outlook on life.

I truly admire how they embraced life with such simplicity. They had a remarkable skill for distinguishing the difference between what they truly *needed* versus what they merely *wanted*—a skill that seems to have dissipated in our modern society. It's sad that we often realize the importance of these core moral values and find fulfillment in such simplicity only when we have abundance in our lives. We often fail to appreciate the inherent generosity of those who, despite facing hardships, had no choice *but* to be charitable and understand the importance of collective effort. In a world driven by materialism and the constant pursuit of *more*, we can learn valuable lessons from those who find contentment in the essentials and prioritize the well-being of others. The ability to appreciate the beauty of simplicity and the value of compassion *should* be cherished and embraced by society as a whole. By doing so, we can foster a sense of connection, empathy, and shared humanity that transcends the contagion of superficial desires and allows us to rediscover the true essence of what it means to live a truly fulfilling life.

Although the country was able to slowly move on with the passing of time, that period in Vietnam was poisoned with alcohol and cigarettes which had inevitably become deeply ingrained in the lives of so many Vietnamese countrymen. The widespread consumption of these vices served as a coping mechanism, albeit an unhealthy one, in the face of the overwhelming anguish and misery caused by the war. The weight of their experiences led to a constant revisiting of the past, perpetuating a cycle of depressing dialogues and emotional turmoil. Even in the Vietnamese American community, the screams of the war echoed. In places like Little Saigon, California, which became a hub for Vietnamese Americans, Vietnam War veterans still gather at coffee shops or bars, reminiscing about the war during all hours of the day. Within this community, there was little space for open discussion of the traumatic experiences or mental health issues associated with war. It was a cultural norm for Vietnamese men to suppress their vulnerabilities and exhibit strength in the face of hardship. Consequently, they often resorted to masking their pain and using these vices as a means of temporary escape, only to repeat the cycle again day after day.

My relatives often brought up stories of my brother, who was just a young child at the time, having to ride his bicycle to pick up our dad on countless nights because he was too intoxicated to even move. While I have not personally witnessed these incidents, the stories have shaped my understanding of the struggles my family faced. I came to realize the immense agony they endured during their time in Vietnam. They always stressed to me how fortunate I was to have dodged those bullets and God forbid I EVER compared the difficulties I faced in my own life in America to the hardships they had to endure. It was considered disrespectful to judge the ways in which they dealt with their grief. They always had a justification. However, unbeknownst to both my family and myself, I would later come to face my own arduous battles in an alternate reality, grappling with circumstances that would shatter my world just as profoundly as their struggles had. The crucial difference was that only *I* would have to live through it, as well as gain the knowledge and comprehension required to find my way out of that hell on my own.

Fast forward.

LAND OF THE FREE

In a nutshell, my dad's eldest brother, Thi, paved the way for my family's journey to the United States. Some of my dad's other siblings found refuge in various corners of the world like Europe and Australia, while my mom's side remained in Vietnam. It was Uncle Thi who settled in Michigan, extending his sponsorship to my family and other relatives, ultimately shaping my family's new beginning.

And so, I came into existence.

Uncle Thi, me and Mom, Dad, brother, and cousin in Michigan

Uncle Thi's introduction to American culture took place in a movie theater, where he watched *Dennis The Menace* for the first time. Little did he realize that his adoration for the movie would have a lasting impact on *my* life. I later discovered that my uncle had named me after the actual character. Funny enough, I was often jokingly referred to as "Dennis The Menace" throughout my childhood. Ironically, as a child, my demeanor was the complete opposite. I was always the quietest kid who possessed an infinite amount of patience, obedience, and respect. Without even realizing it, Uncle Thi had unintentionally jinxed me for the years ahead.

In the back of my mind, I often wondered about the different path my life could have taken if my family had stayed in Michigan. Looking back now, I'm relieved by their decision to move away. The transition from

Vietnam's hot and humid climate to Michigan's cold winters proved to be a tough challenge for my family. The struggle was intensified by the fact that my brother and cousin found themselves to be the only Asian Americans in their ENTIRE school, having them question the social climate as well. The upheaval and unrest that plagued Michigan's cities due to the decline of its once-vibrant industrial sector only compounded the difficulties they faced.

My family longed for a place that could offer the warmth and familiarity they had left behind. That's why we eventually ended up in San Diego, California, a beautiful city on the west coast where my grandma's sister lived. It was there that we embarked on a new chapter, one that would shape the course of my journey.

Upon their arrival in sunny San Diego, my family faced the challenge of adjusting to a new environment. However, their trade skills from Vietnam proved to be a significant advantage in this process. These skills, such as sewing and craftsmanship, did not necessarily require an understanding of the English language, allowing them to continue their work without major language barriers.

While my dad embarked on the journey of improving his English through classes, he was lucky enough to have found employment on an assembly line, working in the production of computer hardware. This job provided stability for our family and became a long-term commitment for my dad, as he remained in the industry until his retirement.

Meanwhile, my mom made a career transition from being a seamstress to becoming a nail technician. This shift was a common choice among Vietnamese women in the United States until this very day. With her dedication, she honed her skills in the nail industry and built a successful career as a nail technician. This transition allowed her to contribute to our family's financial stability and establish herself within the Vietnamese American community.

My family in front of Phước Lộc Thọ (Asian Garden Mall) in Westminster, CA

As we settled into our new lives, it was fortunate that our extended family, including my grandparents and uncles, resided in the same neighborhood. This closeness gave us a strong support system, and I spent much of my early childhood surrounded by their love and care. Their presence gave us a sense of familiarity and belonging, making the transition to a new country easier as a family. During that time, the neighborhood of Linda Vista in San Diego served as a hub for Vietnamese immigrants, allowing my family to gradually adapt to American society. The community not only provided practical help but also served as an emotional support system. Being surrounded by people who understood the challenges of adapting to a new culture helped alleviate any feelings of isolation or alienation. The shared experiences and sense of identity fostered a feeling of belonging and camaraderie within the community. Moreover, the presence of businesses, services, and resources catered to the needs of Vietnamese immigrants in Linda Vista made the transition smoother. Grocery stores stocked with familiar ingredients and cultural organizations offering language classes and cultural events contributed to a sense of continuity and connection to our heritage.

But as time went by, my grandparents ultimately made the decision to relocate to Orange County in 1994, where they would live with my aunt and her new husband. This news tore my heart from my body, and on their final day here, I clung onto my grandma's leg, begging her not to leave, tears streaming down my face as dramatic Vietnamese music blasted in the background in her duplex. Until this very day, my aunts and uncles still tease me about that moment of sorrow.

In front of my grandparent' house in Linda Vista.

With their departure, a void was left in my life. No more coconut

wafers from my grandma's kitchen, no more delightful trips to the grocery store filled with laughter and stories, and no more of that un-conditional love and affection they showered me with daily. At the tender age of four, I experienced my first moment of grief, realizing that cherished moments and loved ones could slip away, leaving an emptiness that was difficult to bear.

However, I was fortunate to be the only "baby nephew" in Cali-fornia, and as a result, my aunts and uncles rallied around me, taking turns in helping raise me during the time they had to live with me in my parents' apartment. They took on the role of my parents, supporting and guiding me as my parents worked day in and day out to establish themselves in this new country, striving for a better life and an honest livelihood. Yet, as my aunts and uncles eventually got married, had children of their own, and moved into their own homes, it was my brother who shouldered the responsibility of nur-turing and shaping my upbringing, becoming the sole presence in my life when others were no longer around.

During my early years, I was a cheerful, shy, and hopeful child. I eagerly waited for my parents to come home from work each and every day. My childhood memories are filled with simple joys like playing in the bathtub, using cardboard boxes to create forts, and discovering unique ways to make the most of the cigarette burns on our carpet (they became makeshift putting holes for our mar-bles). Christmases and birthdays brought immense happiness, even though I only received cheap toys from the 99 Cent Store.

We never used the word "poor" in our family; it was the only life that we knew with nothing else to compare it to. No matter the situation, we approached it with optimism and made the best of what we had. On special occasions like my mom's birthday or Mother's Day, I took pride in making her delicious government cheese sandwiches. On Father's Day, I would draw colorful pictures for my dad on the back of the advertisements that arrived in the mail. I eagerly anticipated the arrival of monthly cereal boxes filled with "luxury" cereals, which provided a break from our usual Kix cereal with added sugar.

I would look through the colorful Christmas catalogs from Sears filled with a buffet of toys and electronics, even though I knew we couldn't afford ANYTHING that lived on those shiny pages. I would spend months browsing over and over, circling every toy that I *had* to have, which only resulted in disappointment on Christmas day. Yet, it still brought me joy knowing that there were kids out there that would be enjoying them, and maybe *one day* one of those kids could be me. I would dream of a future where my parents would be wealthy enough to buy me just *one* toy from those catalogs.

I kept these dreams to myself, understanding the limitations of our resources and not wanting to make them feel bad. Despite being merely a child, I understood the value of money and would sometimes even urge my parents to work less if I promised not to beg for as many gifts. What was truly important to me was really our time spent together as a family.

While my parents were stuck binging Chinese soap operas, I would sit by their side and tell them about my aspirations to become a doctor or a lawyer when I grew up. I vowed to take care of them, give them all my money, and buy them a beautiful house so that we could finally have a garage, a staircase, a backyard– and we would never have to eat leftovers again! We wouldn't have to wait for special occasions to go to restaurants, fear of our car breaking down in the middle of the road, or worry about parking spots at home anymore.

Despite our financial limitations, my parents, in my eyes, were the epitome of success and perfection. I would have considered it a blessing if I were to grow up to become even half as successful as they were. Although life had its imperfections, flaws didn't exist when we were together. They were my heroes.

In all honesty, though, looking back on my life, I have a hazy recollection of the *good times*. There weren't too many if I were to list them. I spent so many years masking tragedy, using the few good moments we had as a way to erase the woes of the truth. My perception of "good" was flawed. I locked those demons in the closet so long ago, yet as I write this I can recall every detail as if it were yesterday.

It's natural for people to remember the low points more vividly than the high points. Failures tend to stand out, overshadowing the successes that deserve equal recognition. Success can only gratify you for so long, while the journey of the struggles force you to remember its lessons.

DRIVING DOWNHILL

Hidden between the intricacies of my dad's life, a delicate thread emerged—a connection that bridged the gap between his past in Vietnam and present existence in the United States. Ironically, his newfound comfort and familiarity in this new land were followed by old habits.. It was during this time that he started getting comfortable enough to begin reverting back to the customs and detrimental habits of the past, as if he was getting pulled back by an invisible force. Every passing day, he surrendered himself to the ritual of shamelessly smoking a whole pack of cigarettes, watching the wisps of smoke dance among his cherished memories and aspirations. As evenings settled in, he sought comfort in rowdy nights spent with his friends. He saw it as his rightful privilege, a tribute to his Vietnamese heritage deeply rooted in *tradition* and *expectation*.

My mom found herself unable to speak freely, her words stifled by societal norms. My brother and I, young and impressionable, were caught in the currents of silent compliance, following the unwritten rules imposed upon us by our culture. Obedience and subservience were expected virtues for Vietnamese women and children, regardless of age. Thus, my mom embraced her silence, her voice muffled for countless years. But as time flowed steadily onward, a transformation took root within her. From the depths of neglect and disregard, her spirit emerged, bringing about inevitable resilience. Year after year, she grew stronger, defying the odds like a flower breaking through hardened soil. She had begun leaving my Dad with a portion of the cooking duties, went out with her friends without him, and called him out whenever he was wrong. She finally fought back against the conditions brought upon us, but more importantly against the spirit who took over the soul of the man I called my dad.

After enduring years in a rat-infested, paint-scorched apartment situated in a rough neighborhood, my mom reached a breaking point and decided she couldn't take it anymore. I was just four years old when she took me on a journey of a walk to an apartment complex managed by one of her nail clients, which happened to be closer to her workplace (little did I know that the walk was an hour long, a detail she failed to mention). I took hesitant steps, my feet sheltered only in flip flops, as we embarked on a journey farther than I had ever walked before. Yet, despite the discomfort, I stayed quiet, observing my mom's fixed expression. Her face reflected a mix of determination and frustration, as if she carried the weight of transforming our lives solely on her shoulders. I took note of the drastic change in scenery as we got closer and closer to our destination. We started off our journey surrounded by run down homes, dead grass, and homeless people on the streets. Yet, only a few miles away, I was greeted by white military families with their children playing freely outside of their homes. It was picture perfect.

A few months later, we found ourselves settling into apartment #60 at the College Gardens Apartments on Linda Vista Road, located just above the manager's unit. Although it was only a five-minute drive from our old apartment complex, the differences were night and day. Little did I know then that this apartment would serve as the backdrop for both the most incredible and challenging moments of my life, leaving me completely unaware of what awaited me.

Back then, our family only owned a boxy, ancient, blue Honda Civic. The driver's side window had to be left slightly open so we could unlock the door using a clothes hanger. Once you were inside, *anyone* could start the car with any key lying around or even a screwdriver, if they were determined enough. It must have gotten stolen at least a dozen times. Since my dad was the only family member licensed to drive, he had to drive my mom to work every day and pick her up afterwards. On the occasions when my dad was too intoxicated to drive after a night out with the boys, my mom had no choice but to walk home from work. If it was too dark for her to walk alone, my brother and I would accompany her on the twenty-minute journey back from the nail shop. As my brother's school schedule became busier, I took on the responsibility of joining her on these walks myself starting from the age of nine. I had to step up and assume the role of the man of the house.

This toxic pattern of neglect persisted for several years. She took on almost every role in our lives and I could hardly remember seeing my dad during those years. My mom's workday began at nine in the morning and ended around seven in the evening. Every Friday, it was my duty to help her clean our apartment. While I wiped down the windows, television, dining table, and decorations, she tackled the bathrooms, kitchen, and floors. Our home may have not been what people would consider a luxurious suite, but it was a place we were proud of. Maintaining it was key. But of course there were nights when exhaustion would overpower her.

There was one night when I had finished my chores of cleaning the windows and washing the dishes. I hurriedly ran and jumped on our old, velvet, flower-patterned sofa to turn on the TV and watch *Are You Afraid of the Dark?* on Nickelodeon while waiting for my mom to finish cleaning the bathrooms so that I could take a bath. After indulging in spooky tales for about an hour, I noticed a deafening silence in the house. Curiously, I walked into my parents' bedroom and found my mom sitting on the bed, staring at the wall. "I'm so exhausted, I think I'm going to faint," she said. Oblivious to her plea for help, I ignored it and assumed she was playing a prank on me. I jumped on the bed repeatedly, trying to get her to stop messing with me, but there was no response. Suddenly, it dawned on me that something was seriously wrong. I reached for the jar of Vicks Vaporub, as if it were instinctive, and rubbed some on my mom's stomach and under her nose, hoping it would revive her.

Surprisingly, she broke free from whatever spell had gripped her. As soon as she regained consciousness, her first words to me were, "How did you know to do that? My sweet baby boy." Overwhelmed with emotion, I cried for an hour, contemplating what I would do if my mom ever died.

REAL CHAOS IS SILENT

Mom and I were nestled in bed, glued to the captivating world of her beloved Korean dramas. Suddenly, a resounding thud echoed through the house as the front door slammed shut. Although we maintained a façade of nonchalance, deep down we anxiously anticipated his entrance, bracing ourselves for what would follow. Time seemed to stretch on endlessly, until finally my dad appeared in the room, after seeming to struggle removing his shoes and scarring down a cigarette in the living room. As we observed his expression, a heavy silence enveloped us. Ignoring our presence, he marched straight to the closet to change. In that moment, we let our guard down, thinking the worst was behind us. Yet, out of nowhere, my dad's demeanor shifted, and he erupted in anger, accusing my mom of staring at him with disgust. Frozen in place, I watched as they had their verbal duel, the intensity of their words escalating with each passing moment. The confrontation spilled over into the kitchen, where the unmistakable sound of shattering glass vases against the laminate floor reverberated through the house. Concerned for my mom's well-being, I broke free from my haven of silence, only to be met with her screams to go back. Hastily, I retreated back to the safety of our room, where I dialed my brother's pager number, hoping he would get the message and call back so that I could vent to him about the imminent danger that loomed before me.

As time passed, the impact of these traumatic episodes gradually dulled within me. It became a part of my existence, numbing my emotions and teaching me the art of compartmentalization. I learned to tuck away those memories, treating them as something ordinary, a distorted benchmark of normalcy. As soon as my dad's episodes concluded, our family would gather the remnants of peace and strive to find our way forward in those fleeting moments. We found peace in directing our attention towards the moments of joy that we were able to conjure, consciously choosing not to let the challenges overshadow these positive experiences.

Regrettably, we allowed ourselves to adapt and accept this unacceptable situation more than we should have. It was an unfortunate reality that we had to face. Seeking help from the police or reporting to Child Protective Services were not even considered viable options for us. Such actions would be seen as a significant loss of respect and dignity in the eyes of our traditional Vietnamese community. Instead, we chose to maintain silence and resolve our conflicts within the confines of our own family. Whether or not you agree with this approach to conflict resolution, it is disconcerting that even today, the majority of Asian Americans in this country continue to face similar challenges.

When my brother finally obtained his driver's license, he became my escape from the chaos. He would whisk me away to Baskin-Robbins for a comforting scoop of ice cream or to the peaceful shores of La Jolla Beach, hoping to distract my attention from the battles that consumed our home. Yet, despite his efforts, my worries persisted, casting a shadow over these temporary fixes. Deep down, I knew that as soon as we arrived back home, I would be faced with the daunting task of sweeping up the remnants of the destruction. And the following morning, I would have to wake up with a smile on my face, putting on a façade as if nothing had ever transpired and carrying on with the weight of the unspoken turmoil that permeated our lives.

I was completely unaware of the long-lasting impact this destructive cycle would have on my personal growth and well-being. The concept of mental health still remains shrouded in silence within Asian societies, rarely acknowledged or discussed, but we are making progress. Pride ran deep, preventing any admission of vulnerability or the attachment of labels such as PTSD or other diagnoses, as they were considered taboo and foolish. Admitting such was simply out of the question. Unfortunately, this cultural inclination to distract oneself from mental health challenges often comes at the expense of those closest to you. Verbal and emotional abuse were not recognized as such, making it difficult to address or seek help for the wounds inflicted upon us.

ANH 2 (ELDEST BROTHER)

As my brother grew older, a sense of calm gradually settled over our household, bringing relief to all of us. Instead of allowing our dad to engage in dangerous behavior like drinking and driving, my brother took on the responsibility of picking him up after his binge drinking sessions. With his increasing maturity and authority, the atmosphere at home became far less tense. It certainly helped that my brother had achieved mastery in martial arts at a young age, commanding respect from our dad. As a result, our dad began to adopt a more reasonable and level-headed approach when facing problems. I was just relieved that their relationship never escalated to the point that physical confrontation became necessary.

He embodied every ideal that Asian parents could ever have for their child. He was a respected community leader who not only taught Chinese lion dance and martial arts but also dedicated his time at the public library teaching English to immigrant children from Vietnam as well as participating as a Vietnamese Boy Scout of America. In high school, he actively participated in the Vietnamese Student Association, excelled in the honors choir, and shone as a track and badminton star. Not only was he athletically gifted and intellectually astute, but he also possessed a calm and composed demeanor that made him well-liked by everyone. It was no surprise that he earned a full-ride scholarship to the University of California, San Diego, to pursue his dream of becoming a physician.

This scholarship was gold to our family, given our immigrant background and the financial challenges we faced. With limited or no credit history, applying for student loans was simply not an option. That is why you often hear some Asian parents being so strict and placing high expectations on their children, demanding nothing less than an "A" grade in their schoolwork. Additionally, Asian parents take immense pride in their children's achievements and eagerly share their accomplishments with anyone who will listen, regardless of the context. My brother undoubtedly became the epitome of a success story.

My experiences with my brother ranged anywhere from incredibly enjoyable to downright dreadful. One day he might have surprised me with a brand new cassette tape to enjoy and the next day he could be forcing me to be the bullseye for his football target practice. But the most dreadful of all was his barbaric way of disciplining me. As I grew older, I came to understand that his strict method of discipline served a greater purpose.

Upon his arrival in San Diego, my brother was unfamiliar with the city's unspoken customs. Like any child in an unfamiliar situation, he had to navigate the challenges that came his way. On his first day of school in the United States, he wore a pair of pink shoes along with whatever shirt and pants he could find within his small collection. Even though he couldn't understand the language, he sensed the discomfort among his classmates as they made jokes. Nevertheless, he remained determined to make the best out of his new life and the opportunities that lay before him. And he did just that, tackling his aspirations with steady determination and achieving remarkable success at every turn.

I owe a great deal of what I know to him, and I looked up to him as a role model. When he started as a wedding singer, I followed suit as his backup singer. Seeing him perform lion dances urged me to teach myself. When he took up football, I played too. He would buy me a pair of shoes that matched his every time, and if he had a favorite sports team, I would cheer for them too. Even though there was a significant twelve-year age gap between us , I tried to impress him by studying his textbooks and pretending to be knowledgeable in those subjects, even if I wasn't really interested. I secretly looked forward to the day I could wear his hand-me-downs. As a result, it seemed only natural for me to aspire to a career in medicine, just like him.

Linda Vista Lion Dancers (my job at the time was Laughing Buddha)

UFC fighter Gary Goodridge once said, "The longer you live in someone's shadow, the longer it takes to cast your own." Little did I know that my relentless pursuit of living up to his ideal would eventually lead to mental anguish. It became a lifelong obsession, constantly searching for a version of myself that could never truly exist or replicate his perfection. This endless comparison eroded my sense of self-worth, casting a shadow over every aspect of my life. It took me a while to accept that each individual is unique and inherently different. Torturing yourself by incessantly comparing yourself to another person and their achievements, or lack thereof, is a pointless endeavor.

As humans, it is ingrained in us to desire what we lack or cannot attain. However, we often overlook the fact that the greatest individuals in history did not achieve greatness by simply following others. They were pioneers in their own right. The ability of a leader to guide others stems from their capacity to lead themselves first. It was only much later in life that I came to realize this fundamental truth.

This predicament of mine was no fault of his. My inclination to be excessively self-critical was an inherent trait within me, perhaps inherited by my dad. At this juncture, I began to dissect dad's daily struggles within his psyche and empathize with the anguish he experienced.

Recognizing that, as an American-born child, I was more susceptible to adopting unfavorable values and principles influenced by my surroundings such as cheating my way to obtain material things that I desired or relying on drugs to take the ease off, my brother wisely took it upon himself to instill the proper values within me before it was too late. He understood the importance of guiding me towards a path of virtue and integrity.

For instance, one of the most ridiculous things he would expect me to do was to read the dictionary each and every day and commit two words and their definitions to memory. This was just one example of the absurd tasks he would assign me. When nighttime arrived, I would have to go over these words with him, define them, and then use them in a sentence (this madness started when I was eight years old). If I could demonstrate my understanding, then I was allowed to go to sleep. Surprisingly, this cruelty actually encouraged me to remember every single word every time except for *one* memorable night.

He had asked me about my two words immediately after I finished my homework and, after expelling all of my mental energy, I simply did not have one clue what the definitions were. He gave me numerous chances over the course of an hour to reach deep within my thoughts and extract this information but I just blanked. He said, "Go sit outside the front door until you remember." I thought he was joking until I saw the seriousness in his eyes. This is when I started to cry and stomped my way to the front door and slammed it shut. I sat there in silence ignoring the echoes of my own cries through the concrete enclosure of the stairs, secretly hoping that my next door neighbor, Colette, would come out to knock on the door and save me. But there was no one to be found at that hour of the night. After what seemed to have been about an hour and a half of digging deep, the words and sentences came to me! My brother opened the front door and as I excitedly shouted the words to him, he replied with a soft smile.

But *that* wasn't all. I was only allowed an hour of screen time each day, so whenever he was out of the house, I'd watch as much TV as I could. I lied a few times, but for some reason, he always seemed to know that I was watching behind his back. Despite my efforts, he continued to call me out on my lies. In retrospect, I see that he was not a mind reader, despite the fact that at the time I was definitely misled by his abilities. Televisions from that era would continue to generate static for some time after being switched off, and the old tube TVs would overheat and remain hot for several hours after being used. I constantly got my ass beat for trying to lie until I finally gave up attempting to outsmart the system. Every day, I was given one hour of freedom to go outside and play with the other kids in the neighborhood. As soon as that hour passed, on the dot, my brother would be found outside the house calling out my name and demanding that I come back inside.

Most of my daily routine was dedicated to homework. And I made damn sure that I would do that homework so well that I would never have to ask for his help. Because guess what happened when I did? If I had even *one* problem in math that I struggled to understand, my brother would help me with that problem, THEN task me with ten more similar problems on the side to solve to ensure that I would never have trouble with that subject again. It didn't matter if I couldn't understand it until

1 a.m. He would sit there with me until I was flawless. This was both a gift and a curse.

Those experiences, torturing as they were at the time, served as the seeds from which my dedication and eventual success would sprout. Some/many American children that are brought up in today's society have the ironic misfortune of receiving lenient "punishment." When I was a kid, there was no such thing as getting *grounded* from electronics like a phone or tablet if I did anything wrong. As an Asian kid , I had a few different "options" for my actual, physical punishments. My family, as creative as they were, could come up with a variety of innovative and terrible punishments for me, such as making me kneel on the ground for an hour or getting spanked with a chopstick or a feather duster (one time I even had the option of a bamboo staff). There was no means of escape. Cooking, cleaning, taking out the trash, and helping my parents was a ROUTINE and an EXPECTATION, not a punishment. I didn't cuss. I didn't talk back. Because it was expected of me, I always made sure to show respect to every member of my family. In terms of how my family disciplined me, if I could go back, I wouldn't change a thing. After the fact, there was always an explanation and a reason behind *why* I was punished, and they made sure that I always understood why I was being disciplined in the first place. The punishment served its mission and was effective in producing the desired outcomes.

Even though my brother was a father figure to me, I was often alone. This upbringing instilled in me a sense of self-sufficiency. Starting from first grade, I walked to and from school every day, as there were no other options available. Nowadays, the thought of such independence would make most parents anxious. It was a different era back then, when neighbors and even strangers looked out for one another's children, fostering a sense of innocence and community. Everyone in my apartment complex knew one another. Whenever my clumsiness caused me to forget the apartment key, I would simply walk down to the apartment manager's office and she would come up and open the door for me, and the assistant managers Mr. and Mrs. Green treated me like their own grandchild. They greeted me to and from school each and every day while they hot boxed their patio with cigarettes.

The close-knit community I belonged to had its advantages, but it wasn't without its drawbacks. While I felt restricted within my own home, I longed for a sense of rebellion outside its confines.

MISERY LOVES COMPANY

H aving to be creative and innovative wasn't really a choice for me. It was a necessity. However, the level of creativity I had to conjure really depended on the desperation of the situation at hand. While other kids' parents were able to buy them new Halloween costumes every year, I had to reuse mine for three years at a time. This put me in an awkward position when it came down to our costume parades in elementary school. I was the kid who was dressed like a ninja throughout almost the *entirety* of my elementary days, until my costume ripped, while other kids had costumes that kept up with the pop culture of the times. I never complained about it because I didn't want my parents to worry about such an irrational desire. But every Halloween, I would look at those meticulously made scary masks that haunted the pages of the Party City magazines that came in the mail.

On a day when I was able to work up the courage, I asked my brother if he could drive me to Party City just so I could *LOOK* at the masks and costumes. I just wanted to see them in person. When he surprisingly agreed, it gave me a glimmer of hope.

When we arrived, I excitedly walked right over to the display of the intricate rubber masks displayed high up on the walls. Freddy Krueger, Michael Myers from *Halloween*, clown masks–they had it all! I skimmed the price tags at light speed to track down the least expensive one.

"Anh Hai, look at that one! It's only $60! Maybe you could buy it, and I can borrow it from you."

My brother gave a light, repetitive nod. But it wasn't a nod of agreement. It was one that was hiding shame. We both knew that my brother couldn't afford to spend the money from his part-time job (while in college) on a mask. Sensing the situation, I started walking over to the costumes to see if I could find one that he could afford to buy me. I nonchalantly walked down the aisles and picked a few that I liked and asked if I could try them on. He agreed.

After trying on about four of the costumes, my mind was finally starting to absorb the fact that he decided to take me here out of guilt. The truth was, I didn't NEED any of these worthless things.

"I have an idea! How about we just go get some construction paper, and I can try to make my OWN mask!" I suggested.

"That sounds great! Let's go. I'll take you to Target," he responded with relief written all over his face.

As soon as we arrived home, I busted out my mix-matched brands of permanent marker colors and started drawing out my template of Wolverine's mask from the X-Men. After just about thirty minutes, it was ready to cut. I made two holes on the sides to weave through my chain of rubber bands. Then bam! I created the ugliest mask in Halloween history. But time was running out, and we needed to get moving.

My brother drove me to the lavish neighborhood of La Jolla, where some of the richest people in America lived. We parked on a random street, and we pretty much walked up to every single house that had their porch lights on.

The chain of rubber bands was tugging on my hair, ripping the roots from the side of my head while I had my hand gripped tightly on the Vietnamese supermarket grocery bag I had in my hand. It seemed like every time that I rang a doorbell, the house owners all came out with the same look of curiosity on their faces.

"Ohhhh. What are you supposed to be?" one resident said.

"Wolverine from X-Men!" I replied with frustration.

I didn't receive much candy from trick-or-treating that night, but I actually got some money from residents who didn't have any candy. I must have made about twenty dollars that evening. Maybe they saw my mask and felt sorry for me. Who knows?

After yet another disappointing Halloween experience, I decided never to go trick-or-treating again. That was the last time that I wanted to feel left behind.

I had friends from my apartment complex who would walk with me to Ross Elementary and back every single day. We were a diverse group of troublemakers, wandering the streets as if we were already teenagers. Even though we all lived in Section 8 apartments, most of them had more money than my family. I would watch my friends receive scooters, bikes, roller blades, and all kinds of cool stuff throughout the year. They could buy Pokémon cards whenever they wanted. Out of pity, they gave me their extra Pokémon cards that they didn't want . Sometimes, if I was lucky, they would let me ride their bikes for a few minutes, but most of the time, I had to walk drenched in sweat while they rode beside me . In fifth grade, my brother finally saved up enough money to buy me a bike and taught me how to ride. But by then, all my friends had already moved on to scooters. I constantly felt left out. They had brand name bikes like Mongoose and scooters like Razor, while I had some no-name stuff no one knew about. It might sound like I didn't appreciate what I had, but the truth is, the pressures I faced in my neighborhood were much harder than they seemed. I felt desperate.

That's when I came up with some clever ways to hustle.. After I emptied out my Donald Duck coin bank, I spent fifty cents on a Mexican powdered candy called Lucas from the liquor store on my way home from school. I would empty the powder onto a cutting board, cut it into pieces, mix it with sugar, and wrap them in plastic. Then I sold these candy bags for fifty cents each and turned my fifty cent investment into two dollars. I also bought sticky hands and bouncing balls in bulk from Mexican sellers down the street for fifty cents each and sold them to my schoolmates for a dollar each.

I managed to earn enough money to buy the school supplies and art materials I needed to keep up with the other kids. But it took a long time, and I got impatient. So, some of my friends and I came up with a great idea to take things to the next level.

My mom worked at a nail shop in a shopping plaza that I walked past on my way home from school, so I would often stop by to see her. One year, a stationary store opened in the plaza. I think the owner was Russian. One day, my friends and I decided to check it out. As soon as we walked in, the owner told us to leave our backpacks at the door. He wasn't dumb. We looked around, and I ended up buying the cheapest thing he had—an eraser. It made the owner happy and built the rapport that I needed to pull a fast one on him.

We started visiting that store every two weeks and buying those erasers. We became regulars, and it was time to put our plan into action. During our next visit, while the owner was busy talking to Taza and Zab, me and Tony, who wore long sleeves, slipped some pencils up our sleeves. We quickly joined the others with serious faces. We said goodbye to the owner and told him we'd be back soon.

We all laughed as we hurriedly walked to the stoplight, and I felt the rush in my veins. But as I settled down, guilt started overwhelming me. We had just taken things from an old man trying to sell pens and pencils. I acted tough for my friends, but deep inside, I couldn't stop worrying about what would happen if we got caught.

My friends continued taking risks without me occasionally in the next few months. But their luck eventually ran out. One day, they were caught red-handed, and their parents had to pay for what they stole. The news spread throughout the apartment complex. They were marked and no one trusted them anymore. Even my parents didn't let me hang out with them, afraid I'd be influenced by those troublemakers. Little did they know, I was the one behind the whole plan.

During those moments, I discovered the importance of considering the consequences of my desperate actions. A constant inner debate arose, weighing my desires against my genuine needs. What was the worth of my moral compass? Why did society fuel the desire for more than one could attain? The world seemed unjust. Regardless of my sentiments, I had to abide by its rules. I spent the remainder of my childhood cautiously navigating this reality. However, one positive outcome emerged from that situation: it ignited a spark of hustle within me. This new-found drive became an advantage that would guide me through the challenges of this unforgiving world.

JUST A LITTLE

I had difficulty speaking up because I carried a deep-seated fear of imposing on others and becoming a burden. The thought of inconveniencing someone or causing them any trouble filled me with apprehension. As a consequence, I often chose to remain silent instead, keeping my thoughts and needs to myself, and opting for self-reliance rather than reaching out for the support or assistance that I really needed. Whenever I was out with my relatives, I would consistently insist that I wasn't hungry, even if I was. Likewise, when attending parties with my parents that extended late into the night, I would pretend not to be tired when they inquired. Furthermore, when I encountered difficulties with my schoolwork, my instinct was always to tackle the problems on my own, seeking a solution without asking for help. It was a constant battle between my desire to express myself and the worry that doing so would inconvenience others, making it an ongoing internal conflict that I had to navigate as I grew into adulthood and which I am STILL trying to ascertain today. There were certain moments during my youth when I couldn't hide the truth.

My brother worked part-time at the local library on Wednesday evenings and Saturday mornings. Every now and then, he would take me along so I could explore the children's section and read as many books as I could get my hands on. The library staff adored me and watched me grow up over time. I was always mindful of my boundaries, ensuring that I never got too comfortable and did something foolish that could jeopardize my brother's job.

On a particular Wednesday during my summer break, he decided to take me to work with him because he didn't want me sitting around the apartment with nothing to do. The chain of events were per usual. My brother's shift started at four p.m. when he walked me over to the children's section. I quickly grabbed the *Harry Potter and the Sorcerer's Stone* before any other kids could get their hands on it. As I sat there on the plastic chair and tiny round table lost in my reading, I started to hear my bladder yelling at me to let it out. I wasn't one of those kids that needed to go to the restroom once every hour while I was in class, nor was I that way outside of school. My body was usually disciplined, but on this particular day, at this particular time, it seemed to have a mind of its own.

Half an hour passed by, and I struggled to concentrate on the pages in front of me, endlessly rereading the first ten pages. Just as I looked up, I spotted my brother making his way towards me.

"Are you okay?" he asked.

"Yeah, I'm fine," I replied with a straight face.

"Okay, I'll come back to check on you on my break at six," he assured me.

My brother went back to work. After about ten minutes, the coast was clear. I HAD to go. I walked swiftly to the library's public restroom so as to not draw too much attention. As soon as I arrived and had my heart set on pulling that door to euphoria, the world struck me down. Someone was in the restroom and it was locked.

Knowing that I didn't have much time left until I risked a urinary tract infection, I walked toward the front desk to search for my brother so that I could ask for permission to use the staff restroom. I had never just walked in there without him. But he was nowhere to be found. I walked all the way up to the adult section and paced around the room like a lost dog trying to spot SOME semblance of him. Still no luck. I was fucked. I, once again, walked to the public restroom to see if whoever was blowing it up was finished, but it was STILL locked.

I made my way back to the children's section and sat there in defeat, once again pretending to be focused on reading my book. In the back of my mind I really thought I could hold in my pee until my brother's next check-in, but the clock didn't seem like it was moving at all. I was ready to give up. I told myself "maybe if I could just release a little bit of my pee, it'd be enough to hold me off until six. There's no one even here and I'm wearing dark jeans. No one will notice or even care..." So I let my bladder go for literally half a second. With bullet-like precision, I was shooting out a little bit every five minutes. I didn't even care how wet my pants were, as the warmth of my urine kept me from being cold. And the most impressive thing was, I was *lowkey peeing* myself with a straight face, just in case anybody walked by.

To my surprise, I suddenly felt a lot better! But that's because I had unknowingly released my whole damn bladder and a whole hour had passed. But what's done is done, right? Wrong. My brother finally came to check on me at six as he promised. Once again he asked, "You oka– What's that smell?" He sniffed around. "It smells like piss!" he said with a look of disgust.

I looked down at the table and replied, "I was trying to find you the whole time but I couldn't and I really needed to pee and someone was in the bathroom this whole time! I'm sorry. I peed a little bit in my pants."

"Oh my god! Come on. I'm gonna' take you home," he exclaimed while trying to suppress his laughter.

He then walked me to the bathroom to wipe me down. The most ironic part of it all? As we walked up to the restroom, I noticed something. He pushed the lever UP to open the door. I had never thought of that as I was in a state of emergency. The bathroom wasn't locked at all. I had been pushing the lever in the wrong direction the entire time.

FAMILY TIES

My immediate family's role as the "starter kit" for our relatives in America opened the doors to a unique and captivating experience in my life. When my mom's siblings from Vietnam finally arrived, I was around ten years old. However, the language barrier posed an interesting and unusual challenge as my cousins did not understand a lick of English. While my Vietnamese was proficient, I was a far stretch from being considered a master of the Vietnamese language. The presence of my aunts, uncles, and cousins pushed me beyond my limits in comprehending our cultural language and customs. The ability to interact effectively with my people became a cherished blessing, one that many individuals of my generation failed to recognize.

During those years, our two-bedroom apartment became a vibrant hub where four other families resided. Despite the crowded living conditions, I cherished the time I spent with my cousins. We played games, shared laughs, and learned from one another. It was a blast. In this unique situation, I had the opportunity to teach them, as well as my aunts and uncles, a little bit of English and introduce them to the customs and way of life in the United States such as the basic greetings, modern fashion, monetary language, and just the simple things they needed to know to get by. It was during this period that I learned the valuable lesson of humility.

Observing my relatives, who had left their home and ventured into a strange land, striving to build better lives for themselves, filled me with admiration. Witnessing their determination and perseverance, I couldn't help but appreciate the sacrifices my parents had made to support them, just as they had once been supported. Through this experience, I began to understand the significance of family bonds and the strength that comes from helping one another.

As abruptly as they had arrived, after a few years, each family decided to embark on their own separate paths. Though I cherished the times spent with my cousins, mentally, I had to prepare myself to return to reality. The physical distance grew, but their presence remained invaluable, especially during my teenage years when their support would prove indispensable to my survival. My cousins, aunts, and uncles became an integral part of my upbringing.

These experiences humbled me at a time when I was grappling with the complexities of my Vietnamese heritage. At times, I found myself burdened with shame, feeling uneasy about certain aspects of my culture. The mere thought of entering a Vietnamese grocery store with my parents triggered a fear of judgment from my peers. I hesitated to speak my native language in the presence of English speakers, afraid of being misunderstood or mocked. Parent-teacher conferences were awkward as I often served as the translator for my parents, further deepening my sense of unease. Yet, as I reflect upon my early childhood, I realize that this shame was an external construct. It was society's pressures that clouded my perception and cast my culture in a negative light. During the 1990s in the United States, Vietnamese individuals often encountered unfavorable depictions and preconceptions across various sectors of society. Media and popular culture would at times link them to criminal behavior, propagate the notion of a model minority, and strengthen biases concerning language and cultural barriers. Representations of Vietnamese women as passive or exotic added to detrimental gender generalizations, while stories of trauma linked to war confined their portrayal to that of victims. Occasionally, movies and TV shows would present Vietnamese characters in simplistic or adverse manners, contributing to an atmosphere of xenophobia and bias. However, it's essential to note that these portrayals were far from accurate reflections of the Vietnamese-American community's diverse experiences, contributions, and resilience. Efforts by individuals and organizations have worked to challenge these stereotypes and promote a more nuanced understanding of Vietnamese history, culture, and identity, leading to evolving societal attitudes and more accurate representations over time.

With the passing years, I gained invaluable wisdom. I came to understand that being different was not a curse to be carried, but a unique blessing. It granted me a distinctive perspective through which I could perceive the world. I embraced my heritage, letting go of the shackles of shame, and discovered the immense power in celebrating my roots. As I learned more about the history of my family's struggles through the perspective of my relatives and the willpower they harnessed to overcome them, I became proud.

The passage of time brings with it moments of growth, change, and separation. It is an enigma that shapes our lives and relationships, but also provides us with opportunities for growth and appreciation. Through the challenges and joys I experienced with my extended family, I learned the value of cultural exchange, empathy, and the importance of cherishing the connections we form along our journey.

NOTHING WAS THE SAME

As time went on and my relatives achieved new levels of success in the U.S., the dynamic in our family reverted back to how it had been. There were no longer any distractions that could prevent my parents from fighting, and there were also no longer any distractions that I could use to avoid the fighting.

This was around the time that I started middle school, which, if I had to pinpoint, would have to say was the most difficult period of my life. Despite my struggle keeping up in the material department in elementary school, I was able to harness my other skills enough for kids to forget that I was poor, for the most part. But when the reality of middle school set in, I was no longer the popular kid from Ross Elementary School who was a four square champion, a fantastic artist, the kid who knew kung fu, or the boy that every girl had a secret crush on.

When I started attending Montgomery Middle School, which was located in my old neighborhood, I was perceived as an outcast. When I moved out of the hood and into a slightly better neighborhood to apartment #60 on the opposite end of Linda Vista Road, it took me away from the group of friends that I was *supposed to have* in the previous neighborhood. These people saw me as a disruptor to their usual social landscape.

The first year was fairly simple for me since I had my cousins and the pupils of my brother's martial arts school looking out for me and introducing me to everybody. My brother would drop me off at school every day and pick me up. I remember these car rides to school vividly. His old Acura Legend's alternator was damaged so I literally had to hop out of the car while he slowed the car down to two to three miles per hour just so that the car wouldn't shut off. Nevertheless, I thought I was so cool because we always had the subwoofer blasting music, rattling the streets as if we were announcing our arrival each day.

Middle school brought a noticeable change in how things worked.

When I was growing up, my best friends came from all different cultures and backgrounds. In elementary school, I never really focused on what race they were. I often went to my Mexican friend's house, where his family sold delicious Mexican candy from their living room. They always welcomed me with open arms. Whenever his dad saw me walking home from school, he would offer me a ride in their tortilla van. We would nestle up in the back of the van for the ten minute ride home, our butts hurting from the lack of seating, as we had to sit on the aluminum frame of the van's floor. But it did the job. This sense of togetherness was all I knew. As kids, we judged each other based on our interests and abilities. We were all just ordinary kids trying to get through our childhood.

But when middle school came around, I started to feel the separation caused by race. As soon as I entered middle school, the Asian kids only hung out with other Asians, Mexicans stuck with Mexicans, and the smart kids stayed with their own group. It was the first time I didn't know where I really belonged. I tried to hold on to my friends as long as I could, but things were different. I had no choice but to pick a side, or else *everyone* would end up against me.

People made fun of me because I did not have the latest and greatest shoes and clothes (particularly because I was forced to recycle the same outfits throughout the week). "Dennis always wears the same two pairs of jeans every week," said a student sitting three rows behind me in math class. "This fool wears the same damn shoes all year. His Adidas are dirty as fuck," said one of the boys to his friend passing by trying to stare me down during lunch time while I was sitting on the curb wiping down my white Adidas with water from the drinking foundation. Despite the fact that I had built up a protective barrier, I still felt that I was less valuable and less important because of it. I was angry and then began to transfer that negativity onto other people.

On top of that, the news that my brother would soon be moving to Whittier, California, to begin his studies at a medical school was the event that jolted me back to reality. This meant that I would finally have to be *on my own* both at home and at school, and I would have to fend for myself. I didn't realize until much later that my brother had spent an additional two years at UC San Diego prior to starting medical school just to watch out for me a little longer to make sure that I would be okay without him around to protect me and guide me.

A motivational letter I wrote to my brother when I was 11 years old before his departure

The days leading up to his departure, I spent most of my time in bed as I pondered on how my life would be without my brother. He was the person I had shared a room with my entire life; the only person I knew beyond a shadow of a doubt had always put me first above all else; the only person with whom I wanted to share all of my thoughts and dreams as well as all of my concerns and worries. The day had come at last, and I had no idea what I should do at that point. Because I had always followed in his footsteps, I was never put in a position where I had to become my own leader.

My personality started diverging from what he had taught me. For as long as he could, he had made it his mission to shield me from any and all "evil" influences. He protected me from the potential of drug use, gang involvement, and other negative aspects of the environment that we had to call home. He never even allowed anyone to cuss in front of me. In this dangerous world, who would shield me from harm?

Ironically, rather than giving in to my fear of being vulnerable, I unwittingly became everything that he warned me not to be in order to make it through life on the streets. My decline began when I was in the seventh grade. I frequently experienced a feeling of confusing rage that I could not understand. I put kids twice my size to the test and threatened anyone who dared pick on my friends. I challenged anyone who looked at me the wrong way. In retrospect, it's possible that I was attempting to prove something to both the world and myself. Whatever it was, it all boiled down to a matter of "purpose." I had a tough time figuring out what I was here for. I constantly debated on whether it would be more socially advantageous to be the *smartest* or the *dumbest* student in the class, the bully or the victim.

I came to the conclusion that being feared was more important than being loved to survive. This happened back in seventh grade during P.E. Some of us were just clowning around, slapping each other with sweaty t-shirts while changing after our mile run. I aimed my shirt like a slingshot and smacked this kid named Filip. He wasn't a tough guy or a nerd, he was just there. But this time, he had the guts to speak up.

"Fuck you, Dennis. Try that shit again, I dare you. Let's see what happens," he said.

The other kids in the locker room stood silent, waiting for a show. I decided not to give them what they wanted. I laughed it off, grabbed my bag, and walked out, trying to avoid unnecessary conflict with someone that obviously didn't know what I was capable of. But Filip wasn't about to let it go. And to make matters worse, we had the same science class.

He followed me real close, whispering in my ear, "You think that's funny, huh? We got a problem?"

As I walked, I wondered why this idiot was trying so hard to get fucked up. It definitely wasn't worth getting in trouble over. When we got to Mr. Diggs' class, I sat down, staying calm. Filip sat behind me and kept going on.

That's when I lost it. I turned around in my chair, clenched my right fist, and punched him right in the mouth. Blood started drooling down his neck. The other kids at our table were wide-eyed and shocked. Filip had tears streaming down his face.

"I'm gonna tell the teacher right now!" he cried.

"Do that and I'll fucking kill you," I threatened, whispering in his ear. "Go to the fucking bathroom, clean your fucking face and mouth, come back, and shut the fuck up."

I could see the fear in his eyes. He knew I meant it. And he knew I'd end him if he said a word.

Did I experience guilt during that time? Definitely not. It took a tremendous amount of pressure for me to finally burst. I had dedicated most of my life to honing my patience and suppressing the demons that constantly threatened to break free. However, the more I allowed them to surface, even in small increments, the more I felt a sense of empowerment.

I saw Filip ten years later at a Mexican restaurant with his mom. Surprisingly, he greeted me with a smile. "Hey Dennis, I still got the scar in my mouth from when you punched me." He said it like it was some kind of trophy, a smile of satisfaction stretched across his face. I apologized to him for how I had acted in the past.

Middle school was years of complete and utter numbness. And the more I felt it, the less I wanted to feel *anything* at all. Maybe I was just grasping at straws to find something to fill the void.

No matter how hard I tried, I couldn't take in any of the world's happenings or figure out why I felt so empty. I kept trying to tell myself that things weren't as horrible as I made them out to be. I told myself they could always be worse, that no matter what *had* happened in my life, I was fortunate and *should* have been appreciative of the life I had been given. I wanted an answer to my questions, though. I talked to God, I talked to Buddha. But no one answered .

I found myself compelled to immerse in both the internal and external depths of toxicity, all in the pursuit of trying to gain a profound understanding of what constitutes the "ordinary." Within imperfection lies the very essence of perfection. Perhaps, nestled deep within, was a sense of unworthiness to embrace happiness's embrace. I felt as though positivity and joy were beyond my grasp, unable to absorb into the fabric of my being. A reflection, possibly, of exceedingly irrational self-expectations that soared beyond the realm of attainability.

Emptiness is the heaviest burden to carry.

DARK NIGHT OF THE SOUL

I t was a little past midnight, and I was in my bedroom, sitting at the wooden desk in front of the desktop computer that was lit to a blinding intensity. Both of my parents were soundly sleeping in the adjacent room. My AOL Instant Messenger status claimed I was sleeping. The rest of the world had no idea. In front of me was my Xanga blog page that had the suicide note typed out over the course of three pages. My lengthy email to my brother, in which I explained why, was displayed on the other screen. It was my intention to put these messages out into the world only a few moments before I was sure enough of myself to understand that there was no going back.

I was holding the cheap wooden knife up to my throat, squeezing the handle with my sweating palms and staring at my empty carcass in the mirror.I hesitantly made a slow shallow cut at first. It wasn't enough to penetrate my flesh. At this point I realized I didn't have the courage to go out like this. So my obvious solution was to resort to a more complex approach to settle the score in a cleaner, less dramatic or romantic approach. As a seventh grader, I don't know how or where I got the idea for my concoction, but it sounded fucked up enough to me. Ignorantly, I started mixing bleach, Windex, and crushed up Tylenol together to create some type of magic life-ending cocktail. I chugged a cup of it. Then I clicked the "publish" button on the blog, but the pain in my stomach was so intense that it forced me to the ground. I felt like an unseen force was ripping my soul away from my body . I could feel the chemicals burning my gums, deteriorating them down to the root. My entire body was drenched in sweat. I was shivering even though I was sweating profusely. I threw up for a few hours, and the shaking that I suffered seemed to last for days.

Why, you ask? Why did I try to kill myself? My mind was constantly going back and forth between the possibility that this would help my family come back together and the possibility that everyone would be a little bit better off without the financial burden of me. I had the misconception that those who cared about me would be annoyed by my confusion and uncertainty about what I could accomplish in life . I had fantasized about the glorification of my funeral where I would be the highlight of the show. I was rudely roused from these daydreams when my mom knocked on the door in the morning to tell me to get ready for school.. I didn't show up to school that day. My parents would be at work, so they wouldn't know.

After coming to terms with the fact that I had failed, I rushed to my computer in order to remove the blog post. But it was too late.Two of my classmates, Liliana and Rachel, who were up late on that particular night, saw my confession before I had the opportunity to extinguish its existence.

The following day in class, there was an awkward pause between me and the two young girls who had seen my *last words* the day before. I was pulled out of this trance when the principal of the school and the school counselor called all three of us into their office. I was taken into the counselor's office where I was told sternly to have a seat. The counselor's first words were "So you were planning to kill yourself?" I responded in an emotionless tone, "It was just a joke, I would never do that." She must have read the hesitation on my face because she immediately began questioning me about what was going on at home. Being protective of my parents, I defended them and proceeded to tell her how this had nothing to do with them and that they had no clue about any of this. "I was just stressed out and overwhelmed," I said.

The counselor then asked, "Dennis. Are you a danger to yourself? If I let you out of here, are you going to try this again?"

"No," I muttered, trying to protect my parents from the shame and myself from confrontation.

She then explained, "I'm going to have to make a phone call to your parents, you know that, right?" I began to plead and beg her not to. "Please, please call my brother instead. I don't want to stress my parents out. They have enough on their plate. My brother is my legal guardian, please call him instead!" She agreed to contact him instead and made me leave the office. Two hours later, I got pulled out of class. My brother had arrived from Whittier to pick me up.

I would be dishonest if I didn't admit that I was initially very upset that my two classmates snitched me out to the school administration, but in hindsight I know that I would have done the same thing to save a life, regardless of whether it was just a cry for help or not. In the end, I expressed my gratitude to these two individuals for caring enough to risk losing my trust in order to save my life. However, the counselor who was working with me at the time did not make me feel comfortable or make any attempt to guide me in any way. It's possible that it was because I attended a middle school where there were a lot of young criminals, young moms, and other defiant adolescents. It's possible that the guidance counselor was just too numb and too washed up to approach each student as an individual, preferring instead to view them in terms of their social class. Regardless of the justification, I was aware that I could not rely on these people in authoritative positions to watch out for me and protect my interests. Mrs. Martinez, a teacher with whom I am still in contact to this day, is the only teacher who ever showed genuine concern for me and singled me out for individual attention. She had seen a trend of dangerous subject matter in my work while I was in the seventh grade, and she had quietly pulled me aside in class one day and looked me dead in the eye and asked, "Is everything okay, Dennis? You need to let me know if you need anything, okay?" I suppose that my cries for help were just seeping from my pores, and I couldn't control them any longer, which is why I started representing them in my writing. I just couldn't keep them in any longer. The realization that there was someone I did not have to conceal my madness from provided a sense of relief.

Regarding anything having to do with my mental health, I never once brought it up in conversation with my parents. Whether or not I struggled with depression shouldn't have any bearing on my capacity to achieve my academic potential to the fullest. When it came to my responsibilities and the expectations that were placed on me, there was no room for excuses because I was a child of Asian descent. This was the typical procedure for everything. And for me to even announce this vulnerability into existence would mean being seen as a disappointment and a failure to my whole family. Consequently, I had taken in as much of it as I possibly could up until the point where my soul went blank.

When my brother took me out of school that day, we just cruised. There was dead silence in the car until he asked me gently if I was okay. He then took me to get a strawberry blueberry smoothie at 24 Hour Fitness like old times. Then we arrived home before my parents. We sat down at the glass dining table and he questioned me about what was going on. I confessed that the expectations of me had been killing me and I was sick and tired of my parents fighting. I was sick of wondering where I fit in within this world. I was sick of hearing about how poor we were and what we couldn't afford. He then calmed me down and gave me reassurance that he would drop everything whenever I needed him. He even suggested that he would give up medical school to come back home to me if that's what I needed. But of course I didn't want this. The whole point of getting myself into this mess was to finally become less of a bother. Blindly, I gave him my assurance that everything was going to be alright just so the conversation would come to a conclusion. I just wanted it to be over and forgotten.

My brother could always put me at ease with the right words. He was the only member of my family who ever really demonstrated any kind of consistent affection towards me. See, Asian parents aren't the type to give hugs, let you know they missed you, or verbally express their love for you. In certain Asian cultures, there is a strong emphasis on discipline, respect, and doing well in school. Parents in these cultures often focus on instilling a good work ethic and achieving success in their children. Parents may think that showing too much affection can make children too dependent and hinder their future success. That's why they prioritize discipline and doing well in school over expressing emotions. Instead, parents show their love and care by taking care of the family's needs and making sure their children are safe and well.

He kept his promise and, to this day, has never told my parents about my suicide attempt. However, he DID mention to my mom that I had picked up a habit of smoking cigarettes. He had called me out on it because I reeked of the smell on my clothes and couldn't stand my violent coughs during our suicide conversation. He asked, "How did you get the cigarettes?"

I responded nervously, "I stole them from dad's carton. He has so many that I don't think he ever notices."

On any other day, my brother would be beating my ass at this point, but instead he calmly asked, "Are you going to stop?"

I responded, "Of course."

Little did I know my life would get a lot worse when I learned that I had developed chronic bronchitis from my chain smoking in combination with the secondhand smoke from my dad who smoked in the house every single day of my childhood. I didn't think it was that bad as I knew nothing else. Plus, to even speak on the fact that the smoking was bothering me would have been considered disrespectful. I once fanned my face with my hands while I was sitting at the dining table with him, and he slapped me for being "disrespectful" to him. So along the way, I figured if I'm going to die from secondhand smoke anyways, why not see what the fuss is all about?

I suffered from bronchitis from the ages of twelve to fifteen. I coughed uncontrollably from nine or ten at night until about two or three in the morning EVERY SINGLE DAY. Nothing I did could calm it down or pacify it. To avoid disturbing my parents' rest after a hard day at work and upsetting them, I would often walk to the living room and sit alone under a blanket to cough. I developed insomnia from my lack of sleep and my erratic schedule. I feared the night because that's when I was most alone with my thoughts. So instead, I snuck out to hang out with my friends.

CUFFED

Roughly a year after the suicide incident, I was finally beginning to feel like I had a handle on things at school. I got along with everyone, and academically speaking, I was excelling in every single one of my classes. My parents continued to argue with one other on a regular basis, but I had grown used to it, and therefore I had come to accept it.

But then I got arrested.

I was unable to obtain many of the items that my classmates did because my family did not have the financial means to do so. At the beginning of each school year, my parents gave me enough money to buy just ONE new pair of shoes. The one drawback was that we could only use our credit card at Robinsons May, our family's favorite department store. My middle school enforced uniforms, so I could easily blend in by rotating between two outfits every day of the week. But there were countless kids at school wearing outfits and carrying backpacks that Robinson's May didn't stock, and I always felt the need to make up an excuse for where I obtained my own accessories.

All I could think about was how badly I wanted to feel like I belonged somewhere. I was never able to express my desires to my parents because they worked day and night to make sure that there was food on the table. Why on earth would I want to make them feel terrible about themselves over something that was so insignificant? Who was I to be the one to make things more difficult for everyone? As a consequence, I came to the conclusion that I needed to take charge of the circumstance by myself. This is when I first started stealing from stores.

I was able to shoplift like a pro at a couple of Shoe Pavilion stores and Mervyn's stores, which are now known as Kohl's. I would just stroll in with my old clothes and shoes, ask to try on some of theirs, and then walk out the door as quickly as possible. If I felt like being bold on any particular day, I might have even stolen more than one item at a time. But I got cocky. My band of friends and I would brag about what we came up with and talk about how oblivious these places were and how these companies were so rich they didn't need the merchandise anyway.

So on one particular Saturday, a friend picked me up and told me about how there were these shorts he wanted from Mervyn's. I laughed and said, "No problem. I got you. It's easy."

We rode in his sister's 1995 Honda Accord to the nearby Mervyn's. We parked the car, and I started explaining to him, "Okay. We're going to go inside together. We will browse a few things together and then go into fitting rooms. These stores are typically too understaffed to have a person checking you in the fitting room so we'll be good. We're both going to grab huge stacks. I'm going to put on all of the clothes underneath my sweats and then YOU have to actually buy one item so we don't look suspicious." He nodded in agreement.

We proceeded to walk into the store. It was routine. We did exactly what I explained. I pulled off every single tag from the items I brought into the fitting room. I put on the two pairs of shorts, a pair of jeans, and two shirts underneath the sweatpants and the sweater I was wearing and still had some items to carry out for the cameras. I then walked to the register to meet up with him while he checked out. He walked in front of me to the glass front door and opened it to escape to freedom at last. The only thought going through my mind was "Fuckin' idiots don't know what hit 'em."

This thought was interrupted by a hand placed on my shoulder announcing with superiority, "Mervyn's Security. Come with me." I tried to run but he had me tight in his grasp. I looked at my friend and mouthed, "Go!"

I walked the walk of shame to the security office and sat down in that dark, cold room. "So what'd you steal?" the man asked. I snickered, "How do you know if I even stole anything? I don't even know why I'm here." He then forced a serious tone and said, "I've been following you since the moment you stepped foot into the store." He added, "Plus there has been a string of shoplifting in the past few months by what they're describing as Asian kids, so I have a good feeling if I pull up the photos your face will pop up. Tell me if I'm wrong." I paused and snickered. I was caught red-handed.

The rest of my hours spent with this man was torture. Not because he was an asshole, but because he wasn't. It was just unsettling how he could be so calm like this was an everyday thing while I had every worst case scenario playing in my head. He kept questioning me about my friend and whether or not he played a part in this. I kept confirming to him that my friend was not aware of what I was doing. He wanted to lecture me about how older kids were taking advantage of me, yada yada yada. Little did he know, I was the mastermind. The time I spent there felt like forever.

The San Diego Police Department has up to four hours to respond to a shoplifting call. If they don't show up within that time frame, security would have had to legally let me go. As soon as it hit three and a half hours he was saying, "You got thirty minutes. If they don't show up, you're out of here." I was hoping and praying that this would be the case and I would go about my day like nothing ever happened. When the clock hit three hours and forty-five minutes I was sure that I was out of the woods.

But right then I got a rude awakening. A white female officer, about 6'2" brewing with frustration and an agenda to make an example out of me, busted through the door. "What do we have here?" she said. I remained quiet. She then aggressively pulled me up out of the chair with her arm under my armpits and locked the handcuffs over my wrists so tightly that I asked, "Why are they on so tight?" She ignored me.

"Kids like you always think you're so slick," she said.

The security guard proceeded to explain to her what happened and I sat there with a stern face. I couldn't be seen as weak or she would take advantage of it. This woman didn't see me as a human being, so there was no use in trying to plead anyway. I was just a young thug, a no-good delinquent. She probably thought I wasn't raised right and she would make an example of both me and my parents.

"We're gonna' call your parents and see how they feel about it," she said. I didn't give her eye contact at all.

"Go the fuck ahead," I said looking in her eyes with hatred.

As I listened to the phone call, I could hear my mom's surprise and anger. I wondered how my Dad would take this. My family had a lot of pride and wouldn't allow themselves to lose face over a son's foolish actions. I wondered how I would be punished. I wondered whether they were more sad or angry. There was only one way to find out.

The officer then ordered me to walk out to the patrol car with her. Ignorantly and rebelliously, I walked about ten feet in front of her and left her behind. When we arrived at the car, she shoved me in and waited outside for my parents to arrive.

What's appalling is that the friend who was with me was STILL parked in the parking lot observing the situation taking place. I thought to myself, "Is this guy for real? Is he TRYING to get arrested too?"

I watched as Dad's golden Honda Accord turned into the plaza. Mom and Dad pulled up to a parking spot and I watched them get out of the car. I sat there in the police car, pale-faced and frozen. I tried my best to avoid the deafening footsteps of my parents approaching the officer. I am pretty sure that this would be the first time my parents ever had to deal with the police in their lives. I could feel the disappointment in the air. Because although my parents were poor, they still had dignity. I had just defamed my family name. In their philosophy, being poor could rob you of many things, but it must never take away your self-respect, morals, and values. And although I knew this to the core of my existence, I was also too stubborn and too proud to withdraw. I was in too deep.

The first words that came out of the officer's mouth were, "Your son shows no remorse. You need to do a better job parenting. This is America." Hearing that bitch speak to my parents in her slow, condescending English as if my parents were children was enough to get me to explode. I started to lift myself up from the backseat, but my mother's eyes told me to restrain myself.

The cop then got into the patrol car and drove me home to make an example out of me for the whole apartment complex to see. As she forced me to get out of the backseat to uncuff me, I could feel my neighbors watching as if my first time getting arrested was the pay-per-view event that weekend. But I didn't seem to care. I could say that I was probably more ecstatic to finally have my parents' minds off of fighting with one another. Also, those dumbass cops didn't catch me the other four times I pulled this same stunt. So oh well, right?

Upon arriving home, my parents (especially Dad) didn't hold back on telling me what an embarrassment I was, what his family would say if they found out, how he couldn't believe it. My rebellious nature wanted to react, but I kept my mouth shut. After my dad's rant, I could hear my mom's deep sobs in the bedroom. As I went to check on her, she waved me over and asked me, "Why did you do it, son? If you ever want or need anything, you can just ask us or tell us and we will get it for you. You don't ever have to steal. I didn't raise you that way." The best answer I could give her at the time was, "I don't know, Mom."

Before I knew it, Dad couldn't hold his composure and yelled, "I can't believe I have you for a son. If you don't appreciate what you have, get out of my house!" And of course, me being me at that age, I nodded calmly and gave him a slight grin. "Okay. No problem."

I hastily returned to my room to stuff as much as possible into an old, green duffel bag my brother abandoned there. As I did this, a million different thoughts kept popping into my head. The emotions ranged from rage and annoyance to sadness and betrayal. Where could I possibly go? Now what? Both ignorance and indifference kept me from finding out. I was completely freaked out. After I finished getting ready, my mom came in, sobbing and pleading with my dad to reconsider his decision so that I could stay. After an hour of this, I finally gave in and said I was sorry so the torment could end.

I got a phone call a short while later and it turned out that the friend who was with me was dumb enough to have followed behind the patrol car when we were on our way to the apartment complex. He had been waiting outside the whole time. I urged him," Get the fuck out of here, bro. Are you fuckin' stupid? Why did you come here? My parents are gonna' flip shits on you!" This day marked the conclusion of our friendship as he said that I was a "bad influence" on him and he could no longer be friends with me. Keep in mind that I didn't snitch on this guy even a little bit. I was willing to go to jail with that loyalty and take the entire hit to obtain things that HE wanted. And I was the bad influence. Life works in mysterious ways.

As for the rest of the night, it's all a fog. My parents kept this secret from my brother out of concern that he would take me and force me to live with him.

I was oblivious to the fact that my criminal mistake would haunt me throughout the entirety of my teenage years.

The common belief that thieves only steal just because they *can* is completely false. Yes, it was about the excitement and experiencing true vitality, but most importantly it was about the sense of *need,* whether or not that need is justifiable or not. It was the internal need to measure up to society's standards that motivated us to try so hard to obtain what we could not under normal means. Keep in mind that I was in a numb state, searching for meaning, searching for identity. When I was trying to figure out who I was and what I wanted to do with my life, I had to consider all of my possibilities, good and bad alike. But as the years passed, I've come to see that this episode, like my suicide attempt, was a cry for help and attention. It was me testing the world to see where the edge of the cliff was and how close I could get to it without falling off and see who would be there to stop me or catch me if I were to fall. But more importantly, it may have been a parallel trait to my parents' values that had rubbed off on me.

While my dad's alcoholism was the tip of the spear in regards to my parents' differences, he cannot solely be blamed. As hard as my mom worked, she felt the need to relieve herself with some type of hobby. This hobby became "retail therapy." My mom had always been very into fashion, beauty, and overall very *pretty* things. Even when we were dirt poor, she still found a way to look presentable. She even sewed some of her own outfits to measure up to the stars on the big screen. Unfortunately, the pressure of staying relevant in regards to her look took a toll on her. With each passing year she lived in the United States, the more brazen she became in regards to credit card debt. It got way out of hand.

She used to make me take the bus with her to the mall EVERY SINGLE Sunday. We had to take the bus because she knew that my dad wouldn't approve of her going in fear of her spending the money. Also, he was hungover from his drinking on Saturday nights anyways.

When I look back at it, I feel sort of used. My mom would always promise to buy me candy or some type of small toy when I went, but of course it would have to be under twenty dollars all while she was buying $1000 shoes in bulk. I kid you not. If she had trouble deciding what color purse to get, she would buy all of them and put it on a credit card. And if she maxed out her own credit cards, she would use my dad's name to open accounts FOR herself. It was a very dangerous game she was playing.

As I grew up and became financially literate, I eventually discovered that half of my parents' arguments were over bills, specifically Mom's bills. I had wondered why she always wanted me to be the first to get the mail from the mailbox every day. This was to hide the credit card statements and new card arrivals from my dad.

My dad was in charge of most of the paperwork, finances, and other intricacies in the business of our lives. There was no such thing as Credit Karma or online credit checks at the time. You simply had to request credit reports if you wanted to find out. So it was easy to fall out of the loop.

I was stuck between two adults trying to wash away their sorrows with poison. And I was the collateral damage. I was used as a scapegoat, a test dummy. While my dad would drive home drunk from his friends' houses with me in the backseat, I had to lie about the shopping bags I brought into the house for Mom every time we got back from the mall. It was ridiculous. I was constantly getting tossed around and used by these two individuals. No wonder I was fucked up.

Inevitably, my parents had to file bankruptcy.

My brother and I never got a chance to go on trips or anything that resembled a "vacation" growing up because of this financial roller coaster. My family started out poor and became POORER. The system is built this way by design. There are no mandatory classes on financial literacy in the K-12 schools, nor is it ever mandated when people come to this country to chase their American dream. Unfortunately, when you're at the bottom of the totem pole, there isn't a cheat sheet. You have to learn by making the mistakes yourself. Because of this, I didn't get to experience a lot of the things that my peers were privileged enough to take part in as they grew up. While other students were going to Hawai'i for the summer, I never had any plans but to stay home. I had always wanted the experience that I would hear these kids talk about.

I eventually went to Hawai'i for the first time with my wife in 2017. Unbeknownst to her, it was a very emotional experience for me. As a kid, I would draw these tropical scenes over and over, envisioning my escape to this beautiful place someday. I wanted to be normal, I wanted to feel normal. That trip marked the first time where I felt that I had actually gotten somewhere in this life.

THE BEGINNING OF THE END

From a young age, we learn that pleasing our parents and following the rules earn us praise, while going against them brings punishment. We become attached to the positive attention we receive, so we continue doing what others want to keep getting rewarded. However, this fear also makes us pretend to be someone we're not, fearing rejection and the feeling of not being good enough. We end up adopting our parents' beliefs, even if they're flawed. As we grow and start recognizing these flaws, we rebel in order to protect our freedom and individuality. There comes a point in every child's life where something causes the cycle of obedience to break. This was mine.

It was Thanksgiving week. Some tainted calamari I had eaten gave me food poisoning. Around seven in the evening, I called my dad while he was drinking at my uncle's house and complained that I didn't feel well and that I needed them at home. Dad had told me he was on his way to pick up Mom, and that they'd be back at the house as soon as possible. Because I couldn't get out of bed for any reason other than to throw up, I waited there like a corpse. There had been no sign of anyone returning home after an hour, two hours, and three hours. At this point, I was completely drenched in my own sweat. I needed to get in touch with my mom immediately, so I dialed her number. "Where are you guys!?" I pleaded. She replied, "We came back to your uncle's house. We're going out for the night and will return home later." Frustrated, I finally gave up and went to sleep, hoping that I'd magically get better.

Even though I'm neither a deep sleeper nor a light sleeper, for some reason I can always hear my name being called, no matter how faintly it's spoken. I was startled awake at approximately one in the morning by the sound of the front door being slammed. It seemed like my parents might have finally arrived home. I slowed down my breathing and listened more closely because I wanted to confirm. I could make out the sound of someone struggling. The voices started out soft and then got louder and louder. I heard the struggle yet again. Then, to my dismay, I made out a mumbled "Dennis!" My mom called for me three times.

My instincts told me I needed to run out to the living room. We lived in a fairly small apartment, so it took me about seven steps to reach them. I went blank and saw red. I remember seeing my dad's arms beginning to strangle my mom. I wrestled his hands off of her, lifted him up, and body slammed him onto the couch. He was still either too intoxicated or in shock to react. I lifted him up over my shoulders and essentially tackled him to the bedroom and body slammed him onto his bed. "Go to sleep!!" I yelled. I didn't know what came over me, but I kept slamming him over and over onto the bed until my arms gave out. I was a kid, but he was a skinny man so I was able to overpower him. I pinned him down and kept asking him "WHY!?" I didn't even know what I was referring to at the time. I just kept repeating myself. I kept saying "DON'T YOU EVER TOUCH HER AGAIN!! THIS IS THE LAST TIME!!"

This pivotal moment in my life is one that I am most ashamed of and is always difficult for me to relive. The lifelessness in my dad's eyes as I ripped apart our relationship breaks my heart, and I think about it and regret it each and every day. There is no justification for hurting your parents in any way whatsoever, regardless of the differences in anyone's cultural values or beliefs. I had committed the ultimate sin, not religiously or anything of the sort, but morally. Upon reflection, I knew better. Those who were responsible for our upbringing deserve some degree of respect, despite the fact that some of the choices they made may have been less than ideal. But a sick child with numerous years of pent-up frustration and silence created a monster. While I was rampaging, I was ignoring my mom's pleas for me to stop. But I could still feel her horror and confusion. Once I snapped out of it and I felt that Dad had had enough, I walked out of the room. Not a word said.

I lay there in bed trying to catch my breath. I listened in on my parents' conversation through the thin wall. Mom was trying to calm him down. Drunkenly, he muttered that he was going to kill me. I knew he was talking out of his ass but who knew the thoughts that an alcoholic could conjure and justify? The sword hanging on my wall was calling to me, so I grabbed it. I kept it between my wooden desk and the bed. I waited patiently. Those twenty minutes seemed like a century.

I watched my Dad's shadow approach the doorway of my room and turn on the light. "Dennis, come here," he said.

I responded, "What do you want?"

He replied, "Is that how you talk to your Dad now?"

Mom then pleaded with me to come out and talk to him. I gave in and walked out to the living room where he apologized and went on about how hurt he was and how betrayed he felt that his own son would attack him. Honestly, I pretty much ignored every bit of this. He ended up talking himself to sleep. Mom and I checked if he was still breathing. As soon as we were in the clear, she called her sister.

One hour later, my cousin arrived to take us to his house and let Dad sleep it off. This wasn't out of the ordinary. It happened often. Except this time, the day that followed wouldn't be business as usual.

When we arrived at my aunt's house, I greeted them and lay in bed with my cousin. I stared up at the ceiling until the sun rose. And during my journey of spiritual silence, I could hear the conversation that my aunt and my mom were having about me in Vietnamese. All I could hear was, "He must have had so much pent up frustration." "He must have been so tired of it." "He must have been so angry."

We ended up staying at that house until a little after Thanksgiving. I spent those days replaying that night in my head until my eyes rolled back. I was scared to go back to that apartment and worried about what was waiting for me there.

As I walked into the apartment hesitantly, I was appalled to see Dad nonchalantly laying back on the couch watching a football game. He looked back for a quick second to acknowledge our presence then went right back to watching the game. As I walked to my room with my mind flustered by the emotional torment, I couldn't help but feel as though I were going crazy. Did these adults not remember what had just happened?

It seemed as though nobody cared and we carried on as if nothing had changed until a few weeks later. Until the moment when my entire life would alter irrevocably.

ALL GONE

It was a typical day. I woke up, lazy as usual, and crawled from my bed all the way to my mom's room and hopped on her bed to sleep for another fifteen minutes while she did her morning makeup. I hurried to the bathtub as soon as she tapped my shoulder to hurry up and get ready for school. I went to school, and then walked home. It was mom's day off so I knew that she'd be at home trying to conjure up one of my favorite dishes to look forward to like shrimp baguettes or fried chicken wings to eat for dinner after I finished my homework. I walked up the steps to our apartment, my knees feeling like Jell-O from the walk. I slid my backpack off of my shoulder as I listened to the key turn. I opened the door and got ready to greet my delicious surprise dishes and Mom.

I felt a deafening silence. There was no sound of the vent fan from the stove echoing from the kitchen, no wind coming from our sliding glass door to the patio as it was shut for some odd reason. I decided to call out for her. No response. I put down my backpack and went to the restroom to wash my face, as I could taste the salt coming down my face from my journey home. I walked into my parents' room to check if she was sleeping. I saw the bed sheets tucked neatly with no sign of use. I then checked her restroom, which I saw was wide open. I gently walked toward her walk-in closet which was typically decorated with clothes hanging everywhere from the doorknob down to the walls. ALL of my mom's belongings were gone.

I started to second guess myself. I pondered, "No. She wouldn't have left without saying anything. Maybe I'm just not seeing her stuff. Maybe she went on a trip and forgot to tell me."

After an hour of pacing back and forth, I began to panic. I ran over to her best friend's apartment which was in the same complex. I knocked on the door. She opened it. "Have you seen my mom, Cô Hang?" She responded, "No, son. I haven't heard from her. Sorry."

I immediately returned to my apartment and began calling my mom nonstop. After about thirty-five attempts, I made the decision to call my brother to ask if he had any idea about where she could be. He told me he didn't. At this point, I had no idea whether to be concerned or really concerned about the situation. The black leather couch in our living room was silent as I sat there. I was unable to watch TV, completely unable to think, and I was having trouble breathing. In exactly one hour, my dad would walk through the door after a hard day at work; what could I possibly say to him?

I couldn't decide whether I should feel sorry, angry, hurt, or relieved. I was aware that they were having marital problems, but I didn't find anything else successful to use as a reference point for comparison. I had the impression that traditional Vietnamese families were obligated to remain intact through thick and thin, no matter what. My initial assumption was that there was no way that my family could ever become so dysfunctional. The more I thought about it, the more irate I became.

How was it fair that my parents were able to remain together throughout my brother's entire childhood, provide support and encouragement to him, and house him while he lived out his dream and accomplished his goals, but they left me to fend for myself before I had even gotten used to the idea of being a teenager? How could it be fair for them to have the same expectations of me as they did of him when we would be beginning our adult lives with very different foundations and support systems, or, in my case, none at all?

Five o'clock arrived and my dad still was not home. Six came and went. Still no sign. This could only mean that he went out to drink again. This would make the situation a thousand times worse. I spent the whole night bracing for impact. I had no answers for him, no clues, no ideas.

As midnight set in, I heard Dad's car pull up. I rushed to the window just in time to see him hurling himself over the side of the car. He approached slowly but didn't say a word to me as he walked in the door and headed directly to the bedroom. I decided to sneak a peek and discovered that he was sound asleep in bed. He was so drunk he didn't even notice that she was gone.

The next day, I woke up hoping that it was all a nightmare and that she'd call and let us know she had gone to Vietnam to get away and see family. But reality set in as one o'clock approached and I heard Dad's weak voice calling for me as I watched the end of the Saturday morning cartoons. I walked toward his room cautiously and felt a mammoth in the room. "Come lay down next to me," he muttered. I lay by his side and we both looked up at the ceiling in silence. Finally he broke the echoes of nothingness and asked, "Where'd your mom go?" I replied hesitantly, "I don't know, Dad. I've been trying to look for her." I sensed that he had been sobbing.

When I peered at the filing cabinet that belonged to my parents, I also noticed a letter sitting on the very top. It was written in Vietnamese. Because I had taught myself to read Vietnamese to a certain extent, I was able to decipher just enough sentences to understand what it said. My brother had written our dad an ultimatum that was three pages long and enclosed it in a letter. If he persisted in this manner of conduct and did not make any efforts to improve himself, my brother threatened to take me from the house and bring me to live with him instead.

Despite the fact that my dad was a chronic complainer about our family's hardships, I can truthfully say that I've never seen a man so dejected and seemingly defeated. There was no trace of the haughty, unyielding man I remembered standing before me. He had lost everything he had in his previous life, and now he had lost everything he had in this one, too. It was the first time in my life that I actually felt bad for him. I started to feel some of his hopelessness. Life had clearly left his body. His anxiety was evident to me. His voice sounded shaky, lacking its usual strength, and there was no trace of anger in his demeanor. His eyes were tired, barely able to stay open due to the weight of the defeat he had suffered. The tough exterior of anger and frustration that he had tried to portray as a sign of his strong leadership had faded away, showing the real human emotions beneath. He was fully cognizant of the fact that he was solely responsible for this crushing defeat.

That day, I made a pact with myself that I would never again put myself in a position where I could lose someone to the extent that I had lost both of my parents. And from that point forward, this pattern would be the one that would cause me to be the one ending relationships rather than being the one who was "left" in every single relationship I had. I pushed people away before they had the chance to leave me; though I knew that these boundaries would not keep other people out, but rather adversely enclose me to the world.

I didn't get an explanation or any communication from my mom until around three weeks later. I picked up the phone with a tone of hopelessness.

With a slight hesitation, she finally uttered, "Hello. Con đang làm gì?"

"Just sitting here. Where are you, Mom?" I responded as I contained my trembling lips, trying my best to show her strength.

"I'm in Washington D.C. and I will be going to Maryland soon. I want you to come over here and live with me." she explained.

She began telling me how she was sorry and she couldn't tell me until it was all said and done. She was on the East Coast living with my aunt.

She asked with confidence in her voice, "You're going to move here and live with me, right?"

I don't know why or what triggered my impulsive response, but it's as if I was possessed by some sort of message from the world that I replied, "No, Mom."

She was in shock. She asked, "Why? How are you going to live with him? How will you survive there with him?"

In spite of the trauma that this man subjected me to throughout my entire life, the most valuable lesson that I picked up from my family was the instinct to help those who are in need. My mom was undeniably the more powerful of the two, despite the fact that my dad was the one who would always be the one to exemplify his dominance. She was a survivor. In essence, I couldn't be upset that she left because I understood the reason she did it. Even as a young boy, I didn't need an explanation because I lived through it with her. Perhaps because of this, she did not believe that I was too young to deal with the heartbreak that I was experiencing. Perhaps she recognized that I possessed the same resilience as her. I replied, "Mom, you live your life. And you go be happy. I will be fine. Dad NEEDS me more than you do. If he loses me, he'll definitely kill himself." She then started to cry and told me she loved me and always would... and I'd always be welcome if I ever wanted to come back to her.

Deep in my gut, I knew that I was biting off more than I could chew. My mom was the breadwinner in the family for the most part. Although we were still on Section 8, we got to a point where my family had rectified their debts and began to make progress. But it felt as though we were back at square one with only two members left of the tribe in the household.

That Christmas, even with Mom gone, I took the initiative to set up our Christmas tree by myself and wrapped empty boxes to place around the tree (I used to think the tree was much larger, but looking back at photos now, I realize it was just a tabletop tree that we exaggeratedly elevated to give it "presence"). I also managed to get one of those giant popcorn bins to make it look extra festive. Mom and I had always made a big deal out of the holidays. We would shop for the entire extended family and decorate our tiny apartment elaborately. It was the happiest time of the year for me. I wanted to continue the tradition even though she wasn't there so that I could somehow hold onto those memories. For some reason, I had hoped my Dad would appreciate the semblance of normalcy, but I was met with disappointment.

"Why do you even bother putting up that thing? No one will even be here," he said with a frustrated tone.

"I don't know... I just want to do it," I replied, my head down.

On Christmas morning, I rushed to the tree to check if Dad had left me any surprises. All I found were the empty boxes I had placed there and two gifts that my brother had dropped off for me the week before. I sat there and watched *Mickey's Christmas Carol* until Dad woke up. As he walked toward the living room, I noticed he was already dressed in his outdoor clothes.

"Alright. You stay home. I'm going to go hang out at my friend's house for a little bit," he said with a stern tone.

"Okay, Dad," I replied in a monotone.

I spent that Christmas and the next few Christmases in bed, reading *Timeless Christmas Classics* by myself until I fell asleep. I just wanted the holidays to be over. Disappointment had become the new tradition.

In my opinion, the widespread occurrence of family separation in today's society is quite a cause for concern and often overlooked. I am running into more and more people who are suffering the effects of it. Whether it is due to divorce, legal separation, or other circumstances, the impact on families is often underestimated. Unfortunately, the mental health of the child is often neglected as parents navigate the intense and stressful aspects of the situation, such as financial matters, possessions, or custody battles. While this circumstance is not intentional, it contributes to the collateral damage that affects children even after the divorce or separation is finalized. I know this from experience. Constantly adapting to changing circumstances and losing their sense of home can have a profound and lasting impact on children. Moreover, during times of conflict between parents, children are more susceptible to manipulation by one or both parties.

However, it is important to acknowledge that there are situations where removing children from unsafe or abusive environments is necessary for their well-being. My case being one of them. If my mother had not left when she did, there would have been more suffering for the whole family.

SHAME

The cruelest part about my mom leaving us wasn't the physical abandonment, but the fact that I had to lie about it to everyone besides a few of my aunts to whom my mom already confessed the situation. I went to visit my grandparents fairly often, and for about six years I had to keep explaining to them how Mom went to the East Coast to work and she came back every so often to visit. To attend a family event meant to be bombarded with questions about her. I lied and I lied until I almost talked myself into believing it was true. It took quite a few years for everybody to finally get the clue that my mom had left for good and had started a new life. This fight I kept having within myself on whether or not to keep my mouth shut or scream at the world was deeply disturbing. The other awkward part about this "secret" was that for the rest of my middle school years, I got dropped off at my mom's brother's house every morning so that I could walk to school from there, as my dad had to pick up more hours at work so that we could survive now that he was a "single" parent.

I remember every morning getting dropped off at their apartment and smelling delicious family breakfasts. My relatives were so welcoming and my cousins treated me like a sibling. But it got to a point where I may have gotten a little too comfortable and got so used to eating their food that I was too oblivious to realize that I may have been an intrusion. I questioned myself on whether or not it was just an internal construct, but my gut typically sensed those things fairly accurately. I received confirmation when my mom had called to tell me that there were rumors circulating that I wasn't being fed by my dad, and that I may have been overstaying my welcome.

I was worried about my parents' reputation. The worst thing that could happen to an Asian family was losing face. I wanted to be sure that there would be no rumors of my dad not being able to feed and take care of his own son. So I started to lie and tell them every morning and lunchtime that I wasn't hungry. After a year or so, I told my dad I would rather walk to school and walk back home myself even if it took an hour and the distance was ridiculous. I made a conscious effort to conceal the true reason for keeping my distance from them. I didn't want to create an uncomfortable situation where they might feel indebted to my family for providing them housing when they first arrived in America nor did I want my dad to feel guilty or lose face. I treated them no differently, but I definitely maintained a certain distance that persists to this day.

When Mom left, our finances hit a dead end once again. My parents had never really spoken to me about what they made or what they owed.

I had just been nosy enough to eavesdrop most of my life. And I came to the conclusion that since we were still on Section 8 housing this meant things weren't thriving. I didn't want my Dad to feel like any less of a man or a dad. So that meant I had to be ready to endure a little suffering for the years to come.

When Mom left, my dad began losing his way; he lost his purpose. I, being in the same household, felt like more of a "presence" rather than another living soul. He had stopped eating, smiling, and just let himself go. He would barely cook, and I came and went as I pleased without a word. I took advantage of this because this was my time to escape and go do dumb shit. I snuck out most nights with no consequences. I even left for days at a time without a peep of resistance. This neglect would have its benefits, but I would feel the costs of it as well. Truth be told, I only ate maybe once every two or three days for many of those teenage years. There was a deeply memorable time where I went so long without food that there were tears running down my cheeks. But I was too prideful to tell anyone about this. I would save my lunch from school and tuck it neatly in my backpack so that I could ration it out so that Dad could save money. I always put on a smile and assured him that I was fine each and every day. It was only when Mom called every now and then to check up on me to ask me what was being cooked at home when she noticed a suspicious pattern. She then started sending me a little money in secret once every few months when she had the means. Dad tried his best to provide me with twenty dollars a week and somehow expected a modern teenager to survive off of that. But I understand that this was all he had to give. I even recall how he would take trips to Vietnam about once a year for a span of a month and I was left to survive off of two hundred dollars. Money was the issue that had always haunted my family.

Although we didn't have much, I learned to appreciate the little acts of kindness that my Dad started to show. He would sometimes come home with Coca Cola or root beer and be so happy to let me know that it was there for me. He would offer me his last bag of pork rinds that he had to go with his beer. When he could, he would cook up a mean steak or pork chop because he knew I loved it. Today, whenever I feel unappreciative of what I have or start to let my ego take over, I think back to these moments that were so simple yet held so much joy. But then reality kicks in and it reminds me of why I would never wish that life on anybody.

I lived in a fairly poor neighborhood, so it was easy to find another kid that shared the same circumstances as me. My broke friends and I put our fifty cents together to turn it into a dollar just to walk to KFC to get a one-dollar chicken sandwich and split it in half when we felt like "splurging." This was our reality. But it didn't mean that it was the way that things were supposed to be. I vividly remember the moment that turned things around for me–when I said enough was enough.

One of my friends (who was just as broke as I was) came over because he had just stolen a slab of rib eye steak from Food 4 Less. We were beyond ecstatic, ready to have a real proper, fancy meal. We marinated that thing with all of our hearts, hopes, and dreams. We watched it sizzle in the pan and took in the aroma. Of course we had to pair it with white rice. That was a given. So I proceeded to open up the rice pot. Not only had the rice been sitting there for the last four days so it was definitely spoiled, but it had also become a home to a fat cockroach. But this was the last of the rice, and we had no money. Beggars can't be choosers. So what choice did we have? We took a pair of wooden chopsticks and removed the cockroach with surgical precision. The legs were still kicking. I anxiously tossed it down the drain. We warmed up the rice in the microwave and tried our best to enjoy our luxurious meal.

SET TRIP

My father was away in Orange County for the weekend, so I decided to have the homies over for some beers. After jacking a cart full of necessities from Food 4 Less and walking out, we had everything we needed for a good BBQ and drink-up. We kicked back until the early hours of the morning, reminiscing about our knucklehead past. We were bored and restless, waiting for the next piece of drama to pop off. It was as if the universe heard our prayers when my friend Q received a phone call around noon the next day. After he hung up, he got us all together.

"Let's go. Some guy and his uncle just showed up at Bao's front door tryna' call him out," he said calmly.

We quickly got ready, putting on our battle gear. I grabbed my black batting gloves, pulled on my Dickies shorts, a fresh t-shirt, long socks, and my Nike Cortez. I was hyped for the mission.

Q shouted, "Dennis, you got any weapons up in here?"

"Don't trip, I got you. Go wait for me in the car," I replied.

Having a background in martial arts, I had an arsenal of weapons at my disposal, more than a movie set. Whether it was nunchucks, ninja stars, bamboo staffs, or broadswords, I had them all. I gripped the handles of all the sharp weapons that my small hands could carry and rushed down to the car, where four of my friends were waiting impatiently. The look on all their faces was priceless.

"Are you fuckin' crazy, bro?" all the boys yelled in harmony. I shrugged my shoulders, realizing their disapproval. I hurried back up to my apartment, leaving behind the oversized weapons, and settled for just two pocket knives and a butcher knife. I wrapped the butcher knife in paper towels, secured it with a rubber band, and placed it in a shopping bag.

We started our expedition to East San Diego and arrived at the apartment complex where our friend was being confronted by a rival gang member. We parked the car about twenty yards away from the front door, just in case things went south and bullets started flying. Two of my guys got out of the car and made their way to the door, where Bao was seen in a heated argument with a vaguely familiar face. I recalled encountering him once while helping my cousin with his weekend job at the San Diego Union Tribune prep center, where he mentioned how his uncle was a "big time gangster." It was laughable at best.

The only ones left waiting in the car were my friend who was the driver and myself. We were growing restless. It seemed like Bao and the other guy would never get down to business. Nonetheless, I put on my batting gloves, ready to rumble.

Suddenly, out of the corner of my left eye, I caught sight of a figure in the triangular window at the rear. In an instant, everything seemed to move in slow motion. An older man appeared to the side of me, raised his hand, holding a gleaming object aimed directly at me through my open window. Like a ninja, I propelled myself forward, attempting to push the object away and shield myself by diving towards the center console between the driver and front passenger seats. Instinctively, my friend hit the gas pedal, and we peeled out. As we sped around the block, the figure became smaller and smaller in the distance. We circled back to pick up the others and bolted out of the neighborhood.

"I can't believe that mother fucker pulled out a machete on you, Dennis!" yelled the driver. My friends were upset and wanted revenge, but I assured them it wasn't worth the trouble. Still in disbelief that my life just flashed before my eyes, I began to feel an unusual and tearing pain on my back. I removed my black tee and discovered a pool of residue within the fabric. It was blood.

The adrenaline must have really gotten me through it because I don't remember any extreme pain whatsoever. I *did* know that I needed to do something about it before it got infected or worse. So I went to my friend's grandmother's house to get it stitched up, avoiding any hospitals.

During my years of delinquency. I really gave no fucks.

As I got older, I became more perceptive and cognizant of my environment. The streets were swarming with thugs, criminals, and drug dealers. Being so far removed from my own family at this point meant that I required someone else to look up to. To compensate, I found great inspiration in the few men and peers around me who were truly there for me at the time. These individuals just happened to be killers, thugs, and hustlers.

Between the ages of twelve and seventeen, I learned how to think like them, act like them, love like them, and hate like them. I would come to know most of them and make enemies out of a few. But regardless of their association with me, I would come to learn something from my experiences with all of them. My standard of hustle–although in part naturally acquired–rose to the surface by watching these individuals and hearing their stories. My sense of loyalty mimicked their undying support for one another, my passion was fueled by their beliefs and justifications in what they did. And my humility was inspired by their motto of never forgetting where you came from. These core principles became the framework for my future.

My teenage years were filled with satisfying chaos. Each and every day was something different. One day I would be chasing a car full of "rival" gangsters down streets with knives, and the next day I would be in another neighborhood about to get slashed by a machete all because I was in the wrong place at the wrong time trying to help someone out that I barely knew. I was in the very cars getting pulled over by the cops at least once a month. I was chased and robbed for my belongings. And I was the witness to hundreds of unnecessary altercations.

Once, as I turned the corner to the boba shop in the busy plaza, to my surprise, my eyes were greeted with about fifteen males outfitted in navy blue attire assembled at the tables outside of the business. I recognized the gang they were from and knew I had no business being there while they claimed the spot for the time being. However, I was already in too deep, and they had already spotted me only twenty steps away. As I proceeded with physical confidence, I had psychological hesitation. As I got closer and closer, I knew that I needed to project my demeanor immediately. They knew who I was and what neighborhood I was from. The real question was, what were they going to do?

I chose the weakest link and scolded him with my eyes as I walked past, but I became distracted as I saw one of the guys who was sitting down, seemingly in charge, flash a gun from the hip of his Dickies khakis. My attention then focused on him. Out of impulse, I got closer to his face and said, "If you're gonna flash that shit at me, you better fuckin' know how to kill me, motherfucker." As I waited for what seemed to be an eternity for his response, all the while hoping he didn't call my bluff, he replied, "Another day. We gonna catch you slippin'."

I then walked into the boba shop as if nothing had happened and waited for my friend to arrive. The entourage left soon after I stepped foot in the door.

I encountered many close calls during my teenage years, and my carelessness never helped the situation. I didn't care about the consequences when it came to the streets. It was different. I only cared about the people directly in my life. All other human beings were enemies. I didn't have anything to lose, and that made me a dangerous variable. I don't know how I survived all of those years, to be honest. I had no problem walking up to somebody's house to knock on their door and call them out for a fight, and I had no problem coming to the rescue when one of my boys needed me. I think that the most dangerous part about my psyche at the time was that I felt like I had nothing more to lose. So with lost hope came carelessness and numbness. I was reckless and ruthless. I would verbally provoke anybody and everybody who stepped foot in front of me with bad intentions. I challenged men that were three times my size and I talked down to men that could have easily killed me. But for some reason I always got lucky. I was a crazy, no nonsense lowlife. But I happened to also unknowingly discipline myself to be a leader–not necessarily a "gang" leader, but maybe, hopefully something more.

What so many people don't realize about kids who are absorbed into gangs and street life is that they don't really have a choice, at least not from their perspective. When you grow up with nothing to lose and everything to gain from a life of crime, along with the societal pressures to level up as a teen, you will do whatever it takes. You are forced to harden yourself from a young age so that you don't break. People make it sound easy to keep yourself out of the streets, but what choice do you have if 90% of your peers belong to that group.

It took me numerous near-death experiences for me to appreciate the gift of life that I was given. Only after traversing the precipice between existence and oblivion did I finally catch a glimpse of potential that held the key to breaking free from the suffocation confines of my own mind. While battling this internal captivity, I embarked on a journey to unearth the answers I sought. A journey which required me to search within myself, a solitary voyage towards the truths that would ultimately pave my path to liberation.

When the excitement of a typical day's events subsided and I was left alone in front of the mirror to face the reality of who I was, I found that the burden of self-awareness was a heavy one. What was the purpose of all of this? Some of the things that I did for cheap thrills were foolish, ridiculous, and a waste of my life.

I recall a particular moment that felt more pathetic than the others. It was lunch time in high school. Some of my friends were going to pick me up right when the end-of-lunch bell rang so that I could easily ditch school amid all of the commotion in the school parking lot. Well, the second bell rang, and then the third (this meant that everyone should have been in their seats in class), and I was still left there dumbfounded in the parking lot which, by the way, was located in front of the security office at school. I called my driver but his phone went to voicemail. I had to make a decision. I could either walk to class or hide under one of the cars in the parking lot and hopefully somehow climb the gate and sneak out. Well, my boys came ten minutes late and there I was laying on my stomach under a Ford Taurus hidden between the endless row of vehicles. Security was actually doing their job that day and golf carted around campus, so my ride had no choice but to bolt out of there. Three class periods passed, and I was still under that stupid car because the golf carts were parked in front of me. After three hours of a back breakingly bad decision, I was able to roll out from underneath the car and walk home. I had missed out on actually learning something for nothing at all.

After this whole ordeal, I had some quiet time to think about the *potential* of the life I had been idealizing, one on the streets. This led me to start having doubts about who I was, what I believed in, why I did what I did, and what my future held. Whenever I went out, I made sure to wear all black or all blue as if it were a statement. I spoke up for my neighborhood as though its reputation mattered halfway across the world. I put my life in danger for people I didn't even know. And I "wanted" to go to jail. For what? To what end? To get my hands on all the food, cars, clothes, and women?

SKIN DEEP

Deep down in my soul, I knew that I needed a change. I didn't want to go to prison with the same people who committed drive-by shootings, broke into people's houses, or were caught with boats full of ecstasy. I needed long money, secure money– money that no one could take away from me. I needed to help my dad more than ever. To that end, I summoned all the initiative and artistry my disturbed mind could muster and embarked on my journey to become an "entrepreneur."

Throughout my life, I had always been skilled at working with my hands in various capacities. When I was a toddler, I used to take apart my Playskool bicycle and then put it back together again every single day. I assisted my dad in disassembling the vacuum cleaner in order to remove all of the hair from it. For fun, I'd disassemble and reassemble my inexpensive RC cars. Consequently, I reasoned, rather than wasting that interest, why not capitalize on it?

Whatever it was that anyone needed, I provided it. I'm not even joking when I say that I used to cut men's and women's hair, install car stereos, and even tried my hand at rapping and singing, but none of these things were successful because they lacked consistency. Until one day I had a revelation to return to my first love–the arts. Specifically, tattoo art.

I didn't really give a thought to tattoos until I was about fifteen years old. I had begun escalating my associations with some real older gangsters and started to frequent tattoo artists' houses. The Asian tattoo community was quite small at the time. There were only a handful of Asian tattoo artists and they were the ones who tattooed all the Asians in San Diego. Tattoo culture hadn't quite yet become a melting pot that included Southeast Asians. One of these tattoo artists happened to be someone I knew. I referred so many people to him, all underage with their parents' money, that he offered me a great deal for a full back tattoo. I wanted the classic image of the Chinese 8 horses on my back in a kind of brush stroke style. But at that age, I wouldn't be able to come up with $700 for the life of me. I hustled and hustled but the haircuts and car stereo installs only made me enough to buy food and necessities. After a few months, I gave up on this dream of a back tattoo.

Despite the social stigma surrounding tattoos in Vietnamese society, I was always attracted to them growing up. I couldn't mention that to my family, though, because of the backlash that I feared from even speaking on the subject. They were perceived as the scars of the hopeless– the criminals, rebels, and savages. But I believed tattoos added presence, mystery, and charisma to the individual. Outside of my brother, who doesn't have any tattoos, all of the adult male role models I admired most had at least a few carved on their bodies.

On a random car ride with one of my older friends on a sunny day, I approached him guiltily. "Anh Viet, do you think you could give me a small tattoo?" Given that I was only twelve years old at the time, he respectfully declined and let me down gently. So me being me, I decided that I was going to make this happen one way or another.

A few months later, out of desperation I decided to dig into my piggy bank full of pennies and took a bus to the Michaels arts and crafts store. I contemplated for days what it would take for me to make this happen and came to the realization that all I would need is some type of ink and a needle. Simple. So I walked up and down the aisles and got a set of different sized sewing needles, a bottle of GREEN acrylic paint, and a bottle of calligraphy ink just in case. Keep in mind that during this era, tattoo pigments were not as advanced so most tattoos that you saw out in the real world faded to either green or blue. I was too young and lacked the common sense to realize that this "tattoo ink" was actually supposed to be black. I checked out of the store and rushed home as quickly as I could.

I spent all day looking at magazines for designs that I could potentially draw on myself, and as soon as Dad was asleep, I prepared my tools. Of course I had to be sterile and safe, so I bathed the needle in a plastic Tupperware container filled with rubbing alcohol. The consistency of the green acrylic paint was too thick when I squeezed it out of the bottle onto a paper plate, so I got innovative. I prepared a kettle full of boiling water and carefully poured a small amount of it into a glass cup that was partially filled with the paint. Then, I added rubbing alcohol to that cocktail just because it felt right.

This was my moment. I decided to give myself a classic "Vietnamese gangster" tattoo: four symmetrical dots forming a square complemented with a centered dot (quincunx) representing Tình (love), Tiền (money), Tù (jail), Tội (crime), and Thù (revenge). I had seen all of my "OGs" wear this proudly so I thought it was the perfect starter tattoo. At least ten times, I sketched out the pattern with a blue ballpoint pen to ensure that it was the right size and symmetry.

I took the shiny silver needle and smoked it in the silky dark green liquid. Then hesitantly, I sunk the needle into where the first dot was supposed to be. Nothing. I just couldn't bring myself to hurt myself. I would have to take my mind into a different space in order to get this done. After about twenty minutes of confusion, I gave it another attempt. I dug the needle in and twisted it like a cotton swab until it penetrated. I repeated this step five times until I got a somewhat decent size of dots. It wasn't perfect but I was satisfied and I didn't want to keep going.

When the tattoo healed, it was barely visible. I even had to buy some fine-tipped green Sharpie markers in order to do fillers when I tried to show it off. The lack of contrast actually worked to my advantage because my family would have killed me if they found out. So I wore that tiny tattoo proudly for the next few years. I knew it was there. That was all that mattered.

THE COCOON

It was 2005. A year full of technological milestones. The era of reality TV shows, YouTube, and Internet addiction had begun. *Miami Ink* aired that year and exposed ordinary Americans to the process, history, and sentiment of tattoos and tattoo culture. I wasn't aware of it at the time, but this would be the ship that would launch my career to another dimension.

After being discouraged about my missed opportunity at getting a back tattoo, I returned to the idea of tattooing myself. Obviously I couldn't tattoo my back myself, but there was so much other anatomical real estate I could ruin. So once again, working with a budget, I tried a different approach to tattooing that I had learned about from the streets.

I decided to visit the nearest Guitar Center to search for different gauges of guitar string, and had my Afghan friend who taught me how to build handheld fans when I was little assist me in transforming an RC car motor into a tattoo machine. I used a pink eraser from a wooden pencil as the anchor and connection for my guitar string to attach to the motor mount. I slid the guitar string through the sheath of a Bic pen for stability. I then slid a sewing needle through the hole of the Bic pen and linked it to the guitar string to create a master tattooing tool.

This time, I would pay homage to my neighborhood of Linda Vista by trying to tattoo the letters "L.V." on my chest in the style of a Louis Vuitton logo. I used calligraphy ink this time. I connected the wires coming from the motor to a battery pack that I had duct taped to the pen and was amazed that it actually worked. I proceeded to follow the jagged lines that I had drawn on my chest. The pain was MUCH more excruciating than the handheld sewing needle that I could control. I went through it as quickly as I possibly could. Upon looking in the mirror, I was surprised that it was finally there! My first real tattoo, even though I knew it would heal like shit and would fade from the shallow scratches.

I realized that there was something about tattooing, especially on myself, that made me feel alive. It gave me a vision, a goal, and a purpose. Each time that I attempted a tattoo, it pushed me to strive to get better. I never wanted to get proficient enough to tattoo anyone else. I just wanted to do "okay" tattoos on myself. Plus, I wasn't legally of age to get tattooed anyway. So I guess this added another element of rebellion that I savored.

The fusion of pain and transformation made me feel alive. I had complete control and the ability to mold my essence into any form I desired. Like a psychedelic, it forced me to absorb newfound clarity. It became a portal to a realm where reality didn't exist. It became an exploration of the very essence of emotion itself.

Over the next few months, I took things up a notch. I reached out to my older cousin who had a credit card and asked him to order me a tattoo kit from eBay. He thought I was crazy but did it anyway. I waited for what seemed like decades for this eighty dollar tattoo kit from China to arrive. I didn't know a thing about what these machines did, how they worked, or the components that came or didn't come with it. I just hoped that everything that was supposed to be provided to get me started would be there.

When the stainless steel box arrived, I unboxed everything anxiously, only to find disappointment. Everything was in the box EXCEPT tattoo needles. I was so disappointed I might have cried. I told my cousin to reach out to the seller to send the box of assorted needles and they agreed. Fortunately and unexpectedly, it turned out that the needles from the original order were sent separately and arrived a few days later. AND, a few days after that the replacement needles came as well. So essentially, I received these needles that I had no clue how to utilize nor did I understand what these needle numbers and configurations meant. The obvious solution was to just eyeball it, right?

Of course I had to be my own guinea pig once again. So without hesitation, I plugged the power supply into the outlet and saw bright red LED numbers pop up on the broken screen. These numbers would suggest the voltage and speed. I then clipped the cord into the two tiny holes on the back of the tattoo machine. The next component of this trifecta would be the foot pedal that triggered the tattoo machine to run.

I had to adjust and finagle a bunch of the tattoo machine's parts until I heard a slight humming, which then got louder and louder as I loosened the screw. It eventually became a deafening buzz as though a jackhammer was echoing through my kitchen. But the sound was oddly pleasant to my ears.

I decided I would try to tattoo something simple. So I browsed through a tattoo design book that I had acquired from the bookstore and came across some Chinese symbols. I settled on something that everyone needs–the symbol for "love." This was before I knew how to stencil designs with thermal paper so what I settled on at the time was hand drawing this symbol on myself with a ballpoint pen. After I got an accurate enough depiction on myself, it was then time for the moment of truth.

I perused the buffet of needles with hungry eyes hunting for the right sized weapon for the job. I loaded in the thinnest needle I could find, thinking it would be easier to navigate or maybe even be less painful. I was wrong. The pain was so excruciating that I stopped to catch my breath. After a couple of minutes, I went back in and performed the quickest tattoo outline in history. But I didn't just stop there. I decided I would have a go at shading the tattoo as well. It didn't look too difficult from all of the magazine photos. It seemed like it would have been just like how it was on paper. NOPE. I managed to set the record for the ugliest tattoo shading in history. It looked like I had used a pencil to scribble on a piece of paper against a tree trunk. At this point I had convinced myself that this just wasn't meant to be. I would never be able to be a tattoo artist.

But with my luck, the universe decided to give me another crack at it. Fortunately for me, my cousin from France was on vacation and staying at my house for a whole month. As crazy as he was, he decided he wanted to become my first living, breathing victim.

He, too, decided to play tattoo roulette and choose a Chinese symbol out of my little book. For some reason he chose "energy." Why? To this day I still ask myself. We decided to place it on his chest. Whatever happened after this is a blur. All I know is that the tattoo still looks good to this day. It made me realize my potential and sparked my hope of the possibility of becoming a tattoo master. For some reason, all the nerves and the anxiety were alleviated when it came to me putting ink onto someone else. I realized that it was a form of escape for me. I was in an alternate reality where it was just me, the art, and the journey to the result. I became addicted to this feeling.

If I had given up after my first attempt, I would have never found this outlet. People don't realize that it's okay to try and fail. It's much better than not trying at all and wondering what could have been. To spend time worrying about outcomes that could be rather than using that same sacred time and energy to produce the outcome you want with all of your efforts is irrational. It's simple. You don't know until you try. But you can't just try. You have to be absolutely sure that you have failed in every angle, every aspect, and every approach before you let go of the pipe dream and move on.

My philosophy was simple when it came to business. I would never be selfish enough to risk somebody else before I risked myself. This applied to cutting hair, fixing car stereos, and tattooing. I ruined myself and my own belongings to catapult myself into confidence. I sacrificed every bit of skin that I could reach.

From the ages of fifteen to eighteen years old, I tattooed myself almost every single night. I waited until Dad was asleep, then I would grab my laptop and my little stainless steel box and sit on the bathroom floor in front of the mirror behind the door. I would lay plastic on the old vinyl floors so that the ink would splash onto the exposed glue from the parts that were old and peeling away from the wall. I turned on some hardcore gangster rap and went to town.

There were a lot of tattoo artists who were either afraid or not committed enough to put a tattoo on themselves. But it is my belief that if you cannot relate to the pain that your client is going through, then you do not deserve the privilege, right, or honor to put them through pain. The pain creates a bond between you and your client. It promotes empathy and sympathy and helps you as a tattoo artist understand how to control and comfort your client based on body location through personal experience. Without this, the spirit of the tattoo is non-existent and soulless. I remember each and every client because of this gift.

I've tattooed both of my legs from my ankles up to my thighs, both my chest and stomach, my whole left sleeve and left hand. This was a big deal at the time as I was still in high school and came from a somewhat traditional Vietnamese family in which tattooing was still considered a taboo. The stigma didn't just reign in Asian culture but also, to a similar extent, still existed in America. So with those circumstances, I had no choice but to cover my tattoos at all times while around my family. This meant long-sleeved shirts, sweaters, jackets, and pants in the summer no matter how hot it may have been. I sometimes wore shorts and was able to show my leg tattoos at school, but I always had to bring sweatpants in my backpack just in case.

It goes without saying, I was the most tattooed teenager in high school. Ironically, though, my teachers, counselors, and other school faculty didn't say a word about it. I guess they had more important matters to attend to. Or maybe they were just afraid.

OUT OF SIGHT, OUT OF MIND

My high school years were somewhat of a blur. On one hand, I was in every Honors and AP class imaginable and dominating in every regard. On the other hand, I ditched school way too often and hung out with gangbangers and thugs. I was always the black sheep in those classes because I dressed differently than the rest, acted differently than the rest, and had a different upbringing than the rest. Within my social circle, I was always the most intelligent, book-smart individual in the room. Needless to say, I constantly juggled being an outcast and being "special" interchangeably. I often questioned which traits would benefit me most on the journey toward my future so that I could learn to amplify them. I came to later find out that it would ultimately be a combination of everything.

I had learned to manipulate time and deceive all of the spectators. I was a normal high school student by day, tattoo artist by night. There was never a time when one persona would interfere with the other. I maintained my perfect grade point average and even participated in volunteer work and sports, all while running an underground tattoo operation out of my bedroom. And no one knew or suspected a thing. During this time, I mastered time management, prioritization, and the art of procrastination.

It wasn't until my dad got laid off from his job that things had to take a sharp turn in regard to the balance of my teenage life. It was time for me to step up. My first instinct was to try to get a part-time job so that he would no longer have to worry about providing for me and could focus on taking care of himself. However, I was met with karma. I specifically remember one particular job interview because of the frustration that it caused me and the chain reaction that followed.

It was a hot day. I woke up, put on a polo shirt, the least baggy jeans I owned, and whatever shoes I had for that year. I walked to the Target near my apartment complex with no expectations but with a satisfactory amount of optimism. I thought to myself that all of these chain stores and fast food establishments ran off of the labor of hardworking teenagers so why WOULDN'T they take me, right? It was destined to be smooth sailing. So after that dreadful walk, I entered the store and was saved by the air conditioning. I walked up nervously to the Customer Service desk and politely asked whether or not they were hiring. An employee responded "yes" and handed me an application. I sat there next to the popcorn machine and filled it out in less than ten minutes. I then handed it back to the employee. He informed me that I would get a call with a response within two weeks. I then painfully walked back home in the blistering sun. About three weeks later, I received a phone call. Target wanted to perform an in-person interview so that they could get to know me better and see if I was "a good fit" for their team. I once again took a long walk to the store. I arrived thirty minutes early and was instantly spotted by the interviewer. I followed him to the office which was near the fitting rooms and sat down. This was the first job interview I ever had and I have no clue what I said. But I got the job. The last thing I had to do was fill out a questionnaire about my personal information which I had to do on some system they had stationed in front of the store. Easy, right?

I sat down and went through all of the questions until I read one that gave me sudden pause. "Have you ever been arrested, convicted of a felony or misdemeanor?" Was this a trick question? If I lied and clicked "No," would they find out through a background check? I decided to give them the benefit of the doubt and hope and pray that they would overlook my past mistakes to instead value the fact that I had changed and notice the value of a young man who needed a second chance to prove himself.

Well, they ultimately decided that I was not a "good fit" because my past crimes involved money. I remembers thinking to myself, "Fuck Target. I'm going to buy that place one day."

THE IMPOSTER

U p to that point, I had only tattooed maybe a few of my friends, cousins, and myself. They had all told me to start tattooing as a side gig, and I kept postponing it because honestly I wasn't 100% confident in the skills that I had frankensteined.

When I decided to take that hesitant leap into tattooing as a source of income rather than merely a hobby, I coincidentally and unintentionally discovered my "Imposter Syndrome." Being a self-taught tattoo artist meant that I had no one to point out my mistakes when I made them except for the clients themselves which I was absolutely fearful of. I had no one to critique my art, my techniques, or my approach. The whole foundation of my tattoo education was based on trial and error.

It meant that I could not second guess myself regarding anything I did and I had to maintain my composure and exhibit the most confidence anyone has ever portrayed. I had to express myself both verbally and through body language–the most convincing "professional" stature. This chosen path has come to be widely known and received as the "fake it 'til you make it" approach.

Fake it 'til I made it I did.

The next couple of years consisted of me embracing my "tattoo artist" persona to the next level, and it definitely made waves. During this time, I immersed myself with anything and everything tattoo-related. I went to the library bi-weekly to peruse and dissect every tattoo magazine that I could find to secretly sneak photos of. I decorated every inch of my tiny bedroom's walls with painted Asian scrolls of tigers, dragons, deities, koi fish, pandas–you name it. I even went as far as turning my whole computer desk into a workstation covered in plastic wrap and decorated with all of the sanitary liquids and pigments that I would need for this very serious job of mine.

I tattooed clients on couches, beds, and beach towels before I was able to save up enough money for an actual massage table. I invested every cent I could scrape up into this newfound "profession" of mine. I was even passionate enough–or insane enough, as some might say–to have thrown away the bed that I slept on in order to make room for the massage table.

I've always been an "all in" type of person. It was rare for anyone or anything to stop me or my stubborn agenda when I had made up my mind about anything. And even when resources were scarce, I worked with what I had. You could have walked into my bedroom back then and honestly mistaken it for a private tattoo studio. I never skimped on the details whether it be in regard to aesthetics or sanitation. Just because I was a kid from the hood living in an apartment in the hood tattooing individuals in the hood didn't mean that I had to follow the negative stereotypes nor that my clients deserved less.

I was dedicated to the process. I enjoyed meeting people, the journey, and I basked in the ambiance of the taboo.

I still firmly believe that beggars can't be choosers. And with that being clearly understood meant that I made sure to go above and beyond for my clients. I would pick them up and drive them home after their tattoos were done in exchange for a meal from McDonalds or a measly twenty dollars.

My position on this has never changed. Too often people who start off in the game EXPECT respect without putting in the work. I was a tattoo artist for all, whether you were rich or poor, black or white, gendered or non-binary. I put myself out there without fear of the law because I knew that I was doing everything correctly in every way that I knew how.

Being an artist was, in a way, a vector to immortalize myself. Your thoughts and perceptions are forever engraved onto a human being's body–an image that will stay with them way past their life's end. It served as a timestamp of the thought processes of the client at the time, marking the milestones in their lives. Being able to take the thoughts that someone has and create an image for them to remember that dream by is truly rewarding.

*My first business card that I created featuring model, Masuimi Max,
printed out on printer paper*

INVASION

I kept looking at the delinquent in the mirror, realizing I was wasting my life. What was I trying to prove? Why was I trying to gain the acceptance of these individuals who may not even be here to have my back in the next few years? Their acceptance didn't pay my bills, and hanging out with them didn't secure my future. I had to dig deep to figure out what I needed to do to make up for the years that I lost being lost. I started to detach myself. I didn't go out as much anymore. It meant losing some friends, but I had to focus on making money and surviving.

Went away to Minnesota for a short while and came back changed

I changed the way I dressed completely. It was a total 180-degree turn. I started wearing Abercrombie & Fitch and Hollister clothes. As a result, I noticed people treating me differently and showing me a different kind of respect. As I got older, this kind of gratification felt like it had more value than the approval of the thugs that I grew up with but I couldn't quite pinpoint why. Maybe this was influenced by movies and the way rebellious individuals have been portrayed throughout history. Every culture and nation has their own image of what a "bad person" looks like. Hence, the way we judge people is buried deep in our genetics.

I wanted to be the anti-hero. AsianAmerican gangs were going through a change during that time. We no longer flaunted our affiliations. It became a time where you couldn't tell the difference between a gangster and a mathematician standing next to each other. We used this to our advantage, blending in with society so we could continue with illegal activities like drug smuggling, gang fights, robberies, and break-ins. Going to prison wasn't cool anymore; it was about not getting caught.

Despite my genuine efforts to change for the better, there always seemed to be incidents that pulled me back into the toxic street life and its culture.

In my last years of high school, another school in a pretty rough neighborhood in southeast San Diego began construction, overhauling their entire school. As a result, the students who attended that school were scattered across other San Diego City Schools. The issue was, this particular school's students were mostly associated with the Bloods gang and my Kearny High School was situated in Linda Vista, which was home to mostly Crips.

When the Bloods arrived, they tried to let it be known, whether it was with their red attire or the tagging in the bathroom stalls or walls in the hallways. It was black on black crimes at first, as the Asians and Mexicans typically didn't approach unless triggered first. But as the months carried on, tensions brewed.

My high school had to implement stricter rules. Once the second bell rang at the beginning of the school day, all the gates were locked and no students were allowed in unless they checked in with the principal's office. There were multiple police officers and security guards scouting the campus at all times. And no student was allowed to wear an outfit that consisted primarily of red or blue. You couldn't have colored shoelaces, socks or any other colored accessories that weren't necessary. Doing so would result in you promptly being sent home or to the P.E. locker room to change into your gym clothes, which you would have to wear for the rest of the school day. But that didn't stop the real ones. They wore their colors under their regular clothing anyways.

When my probation ended, I went back to Kearny High School, a new man, determined to turn over a new leaf. I changed my style, ditching the khakis and plain t-shirts for ripped jeans and fitted screen-printed t-shirts. I wanted to focus on my studies once again.

During lunchtime in the cafeteria, I sat with my close group of friends. We were a tight-knit crew of Asians who had a strong presence in the inner cafeteria. While I was busy forging signatures for my friends' absent slips, I suddenly heard the sound of stomping footsteps approach me. It was my little cousin, his face filled with tears and anger after being attacked in the bathroom just moments ago. It looked as if he had been clobbered in the face a few times.

"This motherfucker just rushed me in the fuckin' bathroom right now," he said while attempting to hold his composure.

"What the fuck? How?" I questioned.

He explained, "I was taking a piss, then all of a sudden I turned around and one of them Bloods fuckin' rushed me. I hadn't even zipped up my pants yet. It's the shirt, motherfucker."

"Where is he?" I asked calmly.

My cousin pointed outside, up a three-step flight of stairs that led to another level of the outdoor cafeteria.

I instantly unlocked my knife and concealed it in my pocket as I rushed out to confront their whole crew. One of my best friends was trying to push me back, but I broke free of his grasp and proceeded. About five of my closest friends walked behind me as I rushed up the steps and made myself known.

"Who the FUCK is the MOTHERFUCKER THAT RUSHED MY LITTLE COUSIN IN THE BATHROOM JUST NOW!?"

No response from anyone.

I noticed a boy who seemed to be the one "in charge" and saw him grabbing batting gloves from his backpack. As I lunged toward him to stab him, my best friend grabbed my arm and yelled, "Principals are coming!" I hopped over the metal poles and ran to the nearest indoor hallway to escape. A few minutes later, I called him to get an update on what was happening. He said, "Me and H are about to go fight those fools behind the bungalows. Don't come. You just got off probation. If you wanna fight, I'm gonna fight for you. You have a lot going for you."

I hung up the phone and urgently ran towards the bungalows. By the time I arrived, both parties had drawn blood. My best friend's face had blood running down from his head, nose, and lips. I escorted him to the bathroom. We got as far as maybe thirty feet when one of the principals in a golf cart raced towards us.

"One of you wanna tell me what happened here?" said the principal with a stern look on her face.

"Nothing," said my friend.

"Your face is bleeding, and you're gonna tell me nothing happened right now?" she asked.

"And what's your story?" she directed at me.

"I don't know what happened. I just saw my friend here bleeding, and I was trying to walk him to the nurse's office," I replied with an educated, angelic demeanor.

"Okay, you can go," she said to me.

I walked off, realizing that my aesthetic transformation had changed my life. It had changed people's perceptions of me, allowing me to get away with just about anything. It's crazy how judgmental people are, basing their judgments solely on what they've familiarized themselves with. Evil has no physical identity; it lives within. Just a few minutes before that principal met me, I was ready to stab somebody out of rage. I was the one to be feared, not my bleeding friend.

As soon as I walked to class, I made the arrangements. I was a friend to the "Linda Vista Trece's" (LV13), the biggest local Mexican gang in our neighborhood. I sat next to Hector, looking at him with a more serious demeanor, contrary to our usual encounters and said, "I need you to take care of something for me, homie. I need you and the boys to handle those fuckin' Bloods. I can't get my hands dirty on this one."

He replied with a smirk of excitement, " I got you, G."

I had accumulated a significant number of owed favors during my high school years. Ironically, most of them were from helping out these gangsters with their schoolwork. I was the only one who could connect with them and explain things in a way they could grasp, and I did it out of love and respect – which goes a long way.

When the final school bell rang, I witnessed around fifteen or twenty Mexican guys boarding the school bus and attacking those kids. Hector nodded at me as he was escorted off the bus by security. To my surprise, they continued to ambush them EVERY SINGLE DAY until the entire group of transfer students had nearly diminished. Peace was restored at the school once again.

As the first semester came to an end, I found myself needing to make up some classes. Despite being a senior in high school, I had missed out on a few sophomore credits due to my frequent absences during that time. Ironically, all of my current senior classes were honors or AP courses, which felt like a joke. I was the top student in my first period AP English class, but then I had to take regular sophomore English with the same teacher for second period. She realized how absurd it was and immediately made me a teacher's aide instead. Additionally, I had to retake a biotechnology class and also became a teacher's aide for that. Remember the transfer students who had left? Only two of them remained, and coincidentally, one of them happened to be in that very biotechnology class.

I left the kid alone, and he avoided making eye contact with me for what seemed like a month or so, while I was busy getting to know the other kids and assisting them with their work. Unfortunately for him, his tendency to goof off in class caught up with him, and our teacher ended up seating him alone at a table in the front of the class, right in front of me. Eventually, a day came when he was forced to ask for my help with a project, and I obliged. As I got to know him and his story, I began to feel sympathy for him. He was just like any other kid from the streets, and it couldn't have been easy for his life to be uprooted and forced to transfer to a new school in an unfamiliar neighborhood where he knew nobody. He showed me respect, and I assured him that he would be left alone with no strings attached.

This encounter helped me realize the uplifting power that forgiveness can bring. It lifted a weight off my shoulders and prevented unnecessary conflicts and harm. It was in that moment that I also understood the importance of being on good terms with everyone if I were to succeed in the professional world. What was the point of accumulating enemies at such an early stage in life, only to spend the rest of my years looking over my shoulder? It was counterproductive. Furthermore, it didn't pay the bills.

My mindset shifted at that very moment. I was no longer trying to prove myself to others but rather to myself. I decided to focus on my financial goals and hustle so relentlessly that I couldn't be outdone.

That kid eventually became my tattoo client and remains one to this very day.

The end of my high school years were spent actually motivating MY-SELF to take my life seriously and set myself up for the path of my real dream (or so I thought) of becoming a doctor. I focused on my studies and strayed away from the negative influences, all while still tattooing on the side to stay afloat.

I am still awestruck by what I was able to accomplish despite how I neglected schooling during my sophomore and junior years. I was able to ultimately graduate high school with honors and also lock in full-ride scholarships to multiple universities. I decided on San Diego State University because it was closer to home. I also knew that I would rather be a top contender at a State University rather than mediocre at a University of California school, so this plan was carefully constructed for the perfect execution of my future.

CROSSROADS

It was the summer of 2008. I was hoping to make good use out of the two months I had off before starting San Diego State University to evolve my tattooing. It was extremely difficult to purchase any decent tattoo equipment because I had to be a registered body art practitioner and actively working in a physical tattoo studio in order to receive these supplies. But I was certain that my skills had surpassed the capabilities of my worn down Chinese-made tattoo machines. I figured I would give eBay and Craigslist a try. I came across a very reputable machine brand and clicked on the ad. Along with the photos of the product, the Myspace page of the owner was displayed. So that I wouldn't miss out on the deal, I quickly messaged this individual.

Unfortunately for me, the machine had been sold. But then came a surprising turn of events. The tattoo artist (let's call him Kyle) had a proposal for me upon taking a glimpse at my tattoos and artwork posted on my page. He and his business partner (let's call him Wyatt) were about to open a tattoo studio within the next few months and they needed an artist to "draw" Asian artwork for them to tattoo. Although this would have been a great way to get my foot in the door of the industry, I respectfully declined because my real goal was to become an apprentice and build my tattoo career the right way. He counter-offered by telling me that I was more than welcome to hang out around the shop and watch them tattoo and they would help me take things to the next level since I had the basics down already. I was sold.

A few days later, I was to drive down to Kyle's house to talk shop and meet the both of them. The "studio" was not ready yet. Although this should have been a red flag, I was optimistic.

I drove down to the apartment complex where Kyle lived. It was a normal looking neighborhood. Nothing alarming. He was in the parking lot waiting for me. I parked my car and got out, making sure to grab my little black binder of drawings for them to peruse and hopefully finalize this opportunity. Kyle was a tall white man, probably almost in his 40s. He had thin slicked back dirty blonde hair. When he smiled I noticed a missing tooth. He looked fairly normal and welcoming. I didn't have anything to worry about. We walked together to the front door and into the room where Wyatt was getting things ready for the studio move-in. He stood up and I noticed he was tall and blonde haired as well. But what really stood out to me was the tattoo of a woodpecker on his stomach, which was in plain view since he was shirtless (whether this was intentional for intimidation purposes I'm unsure). For those of you who don't know, the woodpecker signifies an association with the Peckerwoods Motorcycle Club, or the Aryan Brotherhood, or both. But the optimist in me thought maybe he just really liked woodpeckers. Anyway, we proceeded with introductions and I learned they had both just gotten out of prison not too long ago. Both Wyatt and Kyle had worked at some renowned tattoo shops in San Diego prior to their incarceration. Ironically, they assumed I had gotten locked up for arms dealing since most Asians were going in for that. They were almost disappointed when I assured them that wasn't the case. They proceeded to walk me through the "big things" that were in the works and tried to get me excited about designing some drawings for Peckerwoods MC. I was very naive and oblivious to the white supremacist gang culture because I had not been around it much growing up. But over the course of the next few years, I came to learn more than I needed to.

The meeting didn't take long.

A few weeks later I met both of them at the shop. It was a small studio in a very peculiar medical office building that reeked of marijuana. Neighboring us was a "private" massage studio, a recording studio, a few holistic medicine doctors and some illegal dispensaries. It was definitely an odd combination of businesses. Not only was it a hub for suspicious activity, but the maintenance of the building was a disaster. There was one community thermostat for half of the suites downstairs. The problem was that the temperature control on the thermostat was broken. If we turned on the air conditioning, we had to deal with a non-negotiable sixty degrees. Clients were constantly freezing their asses off. And I, myself, literally had to wear a fur coat in the summer to keep my hands from shaking while in the studio. But regardless of the circumstances, I was beyond excited to see what they had in store for me.

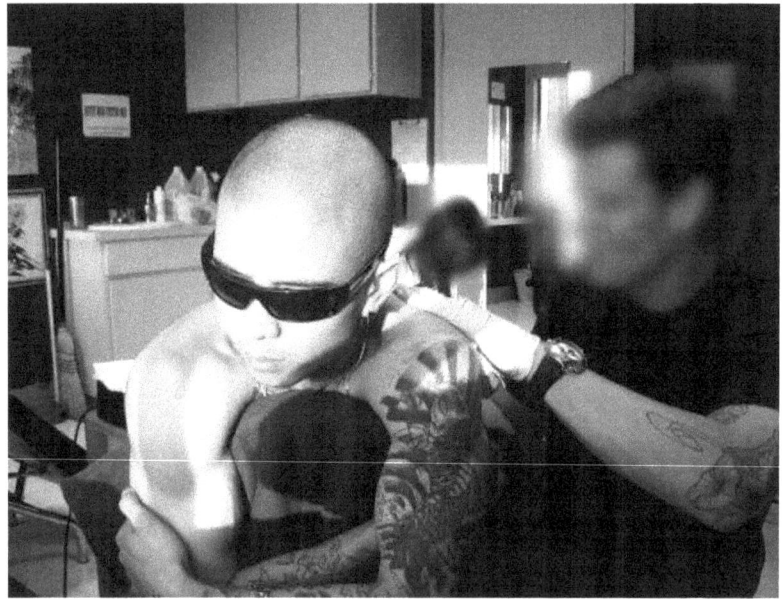

Getting my back tattooed

OVERNIGHT SENSATION

C ollege life for me was more of a chore than an experience that would pave the path towards a brighter future. I had all my classes from morning to noon. Then I would rush to the tattoo studio to help out. Then around ten at night I would finally head home to do my homework until about two or three in the morning and then get a few hours of sleep only to wake up at six again.

I blew most of my living expense money on the most irrational purchases you could imagine like an exhaust and wheels for my car. But I also invested it in better equipment for tattooing. It was the first time in my life that I had more than sixty dollars in my bank account and no class had ever taught me how to manage it.

I had chosen to become a plastic surgeon, but all the classes that I was required to take were preposterously irrelevant: Asian studies, art history, and statistics. A waste of time and use of resources. I found myself at odds with morality and principle. I kept trying to justify the reasoning behind the requirements that oblivious students had to fulfill. Was there an underlying purpose or was it just greed?

I am sure that college was the correct path for many. But it wasn't for me. It wasn't right for my circumstances.

I dropped out of SDSU unannounced in the Winter of 2009. I even had to pay back some of the money for my unauthorized withdrawal. I had no choice but to go all in on this unproven, shaky career as a tattoo artist. I even got my neck tattooed that same day as somewhat of a vow to myself to never look back and to somehow make this only option work.

I was afraid. But deep in my gut I knew that somehow I would make it work. I had nothing else to fall back on. If I amounted to nothing, I would prove the world correct.

When news broke that I had dropped out, someone close to me said, "You ain't ever gonna' nowhere with this tattoo shit." Others just repeatedly asked, "Are you sure?" Some friends called me "stupid" and "irrational." I had convinced my family that I had simply taken a break from college because I landed a job in "graphic design." I didn't want to tell them about the hasty sacrifice I made if it were to amount to nothing. I would have never heard the end of it. I even hid my tattoos from my family for the longest time. If I am being honest, I guess I was ashamed.

Upon reaching this realization, I came to understand that the majority of the individuals I had kept close to me were primarily held onto in order to maintain connection with my mother. However, she was no longer present in my life, prompting me to question why I was clinging to remnants of her and her aspirations for me. It was then that I made a decision to trust my instincts, which ultimately led me to lose touch with many of my family members and friends. Nevertheless, what set this stage of my life apart was my newfound resolve to no longer struggle to retain individuals who did not support me.

Often, those who witnessed our journey from childhood find it challenging to perceive us as anything other than the person we once were. When we undergo a complete transformation, some may argue that we have compromised our principles or values. On the contrary, striving to escape the limitations of our surroundings and immersing ourselves in an environment conducive to personal growth is not an act of selling out. The motivation to pursue our dreams and aspirations should never be misconstrued as such. People can't metabolize change very well.

Surprisingly, all the negativity around me actually fueled me.

You cannot allow the opinions of others to dictate your actions or the manner in which you execute them. Whether it's their praise or their discouragement, remember that they are merely expressing their own subjective viewpoints. It is important not to take it personally. As a person, it's natural to seek the opinions of others when subconsciously you possess a lot of self doubt.

Contemplating the essence of worthiness leaves you questioning whether it originates from internal fulfillment or external validation. Comparing yourself to others who have already determined their worth leads to irrelevant revelations, whereas recognizing your true baseline reveals that you are exactly where you need to be. Often, we become fixated on external perceptions rather than introspection, fueling self-hate.

While aspiring for greater achievements is a good thing, it's also essential to acknowledge that there will always be more to accomplish, and with the journey to success comes inevitable failures. Coping with these setbacks internally is crucial, as others' opinions don't contribute to resolving your struggles.

Your sole objective should be to give your best effort in everything you do. Finding fulfillment in your own willingness to strive will bring you the satisfaction you seek. Ultimately, the only judgment that truly matters is your own assessment of your actions. If you have an inner awareness that you haven't given it your all, the opinions of others merely serve to reinforce what you already know.

It is essential to resist the temptation of letting the opinions of others either inflate or shatter our ego. The ultimate authority in determining our worth resides within ourselves and not in the judgments of others.

This philosophy aligns with the importance of focusing on personal growth and surpassing one's previous self. The true competition lies within oneself, striving to become a better version of who we were yesterday.

Imagine finding yourself in a situation where you face judgment from those within your own community. It can be disheartening to experience a lack of acceptance from individuals who share a similar background or identity, let alone facing challenges with those from different backgrounds.

In such circumstances, it is crucial to remember that acceptance and understanding are not solely dependent on the perceptions of others. Embracing your own worth and recognizing the uniqueness of your individual journey becomes even more important. While it may be difficult, try not to internalize the judgment or let it define your self-worth.

Remember that true acceptance starts from within. Surround yourself with supportive and open-minded individuals who value and appreciate you for who you are. Focus on building your own confidence and finding strength in your own resilience. Ultimately, your worth is not determined by the judgment of others but by your own self-acceptance and self-love.

In today's world, people often form judgments based on the snippets of our lives they see on social media. They create a synopsis of our lives based on these glimpses, which can be misleading and incomplete. However, if you choose to live a life that is truly designed by you and for you, centered around the people you genuinely care about, it becomes unrealistic and impractical to spend hours each day trying to control every narrative that circulates about you. It is impossible to fix every rumor or address every single thing that may be said or speculated about you.

Instead of trying to wash your life clean by over-communicating and constantly clarifying, it's important to focus on living an authentic life with the people you genuinely love and care for. Embrace your true self and let your actions speak for themselves. In the end, you have the power to shape your life and live it authentically. Don't let others' assumptions or judgments define your worth. Focus on cultivating meaningful connections with those who appreciate and understand the real you.

After digging into the shop for a few months, I was able to get the hang of how things ran. I hadn't gotten to tattoo much at the shop since they didn't want to be held liable for me. I, under the suggestion of someone who may or may not have been my boss, was told to continue tattooing my clients at home so that I wouldn't lose my touch and keep tattooing myself for practice.

Tattooing my stomach at the first studio

My moment to shine came when my two bosses attended a tattoo convention in Las Vegas. Honestly they just wanted money to be made that week while they were gone so they decided to vouch for and license me.

They didn't have much in their savings after opening the little studio. I even had to let them borrow my massage table so they could bring it with them to Vegas. I was a team player so I didn't mind. But this is when I started having thoughts such as "Shouldn't they, as leaders, be setting a better example for their mentees?"

Of course, like most business partnerships, the two men had their disagreements in regard to money, fair splits, etc. If I'm being honest, one of my bosses was simply a better tattoo artist than the other and he also specialized in shading which bore the brunt of the tattoo work. They had an arrangement where the lining specialist would line the tattoo while the shading specialist would shade the piece. So we're talking about a 50/50 financial split when the work ratio was realistically 20/80.

When you first decide to start your business, it's perfectly normal to feel fear and unease. The lack of confidence when entering the realm of entrepreneurship can be overwhelming. This is why most people decide to ease that burden, or blame, by searching for a business partner or partners to alleviate those stressors. This route boosts morale and excitement. The success of the collaborative effort is certain to triumph stronger and faster than a solo undertaking, right? In a perfect world, it may be the case. In a business, not so much.

I was sitting alone in the studio by myself one night around ten drawing away under the bright white lights, lost in the sauce when I got startled by loud knocking on the door. I was hesitant to open it, but of course I did anyway because I was "in charge." When I opened it, I was greeted by a young man named Eugene. He had made an appointment to get tattooed by Kyle. Unfortunately for him, Kyle had forgotten about his appointment when planning his trip to the tattoo convention. Eugene was growing impatient over his appointment and asked me compulsively, "Can you do it for me tonight? It's just some roses on my chest."

I gave Kyle a call and told him what the situation was and his immediate response was "Go ahead and handle it."

At this point I didn't know whether I was excited or scared. But I had to project confidence. Eugene knew that I was a newer artist but for some reason he was so nonchalant.

I finally realized the scale of trust that was involved between an artist and his client during the tattoo process. I would never take this for granted or take advantage of it. I would do every single tattoo, no matter how big or how small, with every ounce of enthusiasm and skill that I possessed. Because no matter the cost of the piece or the rationale or reasoning behind it, tattoos stay with individuals until they go to the grave. I would respect the sanctity of this process and hope that it established my role as a significant name in this industry.

To this day, this appointment remains the first and only walk-in appointment I have ever taken. It just so happens that it was quite a large piece for an amateur tattoo artist. He ended up wanting a full chest piece of roses in black and gray and I had only done maybe two roses up to this point. Eugene sat and waited while I drew out his design. I was worried he would grow impatient because it probably took me about an hour just to draw it out. Once he was satisfied with the result, we placed the stencil on him and got right down to it. It took me probably three hours to complete the piece. I became the ultimate hype man of my own work. As soon as I put down the machine, I said, "Damn, this looks good!" Eugene agreed. This artist-client relationship grew into a friendship and Eugene, along with his wife and kids, have been my clients to this very day getting charged the same rate I gave them when I was an amateur artist. I reward loyalty.

But not every client interaction was as rosy as the relationship I was able to establish with Eugene.

DISSED FROM A ROSE

As word got out about my work, I started attracting clients who had no prior connection to me except for being friends on Myspace. Dealing with these social media inquiries took some time to figure out, but I continued to do business with the same values and friendly attitude. I treated every stranger as if they were my closest friend, always being fair, honest, and welcoming. I never, ever pressured anyone into getting a tattoo from me. I didn't ask for deposits or charge clients for creating their designs.

So naturally, you would think that no one would go through the trouble of reaching out to an artist if they weren't serious about getting tattooed right? Wrong.

I eagerly awaited Rose's arrival at seven that evening for her rose tattoo. We had spent several weeks exchanging messages and refining the design until it perfectly matched her vision. After reaching an agreement, I was excited to begin the tattooing process. As a fairly new tattoo artist, it often took me quite a long time to draw out designs because I didn't have a well-rounded muscle memory of subject matter yet. Each one of my drawings were hand drawn with passion and dedication, along with endless research and reference comparisons. No matter how large or how small the project was, I gave it everything I had.

To ensure she didn't forget, I took the initiative to send her a friendly reminder text the day before her appointment.

"Hey, Rose! Don't forget you have an appointment tomorrow at 7. Let me know if you can't make it!"

"I'll be there! I'm excited to finally get it. I've been waiting for this!" she replied.

At seven, I anxiously watched the clock, but to my surprise, there was no sight of anyone in the hallway or any cars pulling into view from my window. I chose to give Rose the benefit of the doubt, thinking, "Maybe she's just caught in traffic and running behind schedule." I resisted the urge to send her a text, opting instead to wait an additional thirty minutes, avoiding any hasty assumptions or potential embarrassment on my part.

Seven-thirty arrived.

I texted her, "Hey! Are you on the way?"

Fifteen minutes later, she replied, "Yes! I'll be there in about thirty minutes!"

"Okay, no worries! Drive safe and I'll see you soon," I texted back.

Thirty minutes passed and still no Rose. I sat there alone in the studio, thinking the worst. Did she get into a car accident? Did she get attacked by someone? What if she parked in the back and something happened to her when she parked?

I waited until nine and decided to check on her once again

"Everything okay? Just want to make sure nothing happened to you. Let me know. We can reschedule if you need to."

I sat there doing nothing until she replied back once again at ten.

"I'm at the ATM! Sorry, it's taking forever!" she wrote.

"It's okay! I'll be here," I replied with draining enthusiasm.

At that point, one of my friends had shown up to keep me company. As I vented to him about the situation, his response off the bat was, "Dude, just go home. She's a flake. She ain't showing up. Why are you even waiting?"

"Naw. She wouldn't do that. We have been preparing for her tattoo for weeks now. Why would she go through all that to just leave me hanging? I'll stay for a little while longer," I replied.

When one rolled around, Rose was still nowhere to be found. Frustrated and disheartened, I reluctantly accepted that it was time to call it a night. As I drove home, a mix of concern and disappointment swirled within me, leaving me puzzled about what could have transpired. Upon reaching my apartment, I prepared to take a shower when suddenly, my phone began to flash with incoming notifications. It was already one-thirty, and to my surprise, Rose had finally reached out to me via text.

"Sorry. I couldn't find a babysitter."

At that point, I completely lost it. I couldn't help but think, "What the fuck?" It made absolutely no damn sense. How the fuck does someone go from being on their way to their appointment to being stuck at the ATM, and then suddenly claiming they had no babysitter, all within a span of six hours? And throughout that entire time, I could have reached out to someone else and filled the slot, ensuring I could put food on my table. The situation left me frustrated beyond belief, questioning the ridiculousness of it all.

Needless to say, I didn't reply.

When entering the service industry, I was well aware that I would face numerous obstacles on my journey. I anticipated the challenges related to running a business and the relentless pursuit of becoming a skilled tattoo artist. What caught me off guard was the unpredictable human element that comes with it all.

Up to that point, I mostly worked on people with whom I was already acquainted . I grew up on word-of-mouth, handshake agreements. It was the covenant of the streets. My trust in humanity was based on a rather limited trial sample.

I had underestimated the capacity for inconsideration, irresponsibility, and disrespect that some individuals possessed. While I endeavored to maintain a positive outlook despite the occasional no-shows, there came a time when a single client failing to appear could have serious consequences, leaving me on the brink of hunger or homelessness.

As a newcomer in the industry, I often encountered potential clients who seemed to believe they were doing me a favor by allowing me to work on them. They were willing to let me "practice" on them. There were many people who wanted free work and pretended it was a favor. They made empty promises of promoting me and helping me gain recognition for my talents. As a naive and young artist, I was inclined to believe them.

Meeting celebrities, athletes, and public figures can lead to the assumption that being associated with them will bring benefits. It's natural to have the desire to treat them with utmost respect and offer your services for free, hoping to have a small impact on their lives. But would you still do all of that if you knew they didn't value or appreciate your work?

Genuine individuals who truly appreciate your creations will be willing to pay, even if you don't ask for it. They will insist on supporting your dreams and helping you sustain yourself. Anyone who genuinely respects you and your work would never let you dedicate hours of your time without the basic understanding of compensating you for your efforts, not to mention your valuable time.

Speaking from experience, I will tell you that the random, humble engineer that you cross paths with and work on will pay you what you're worth without hesitation. Without a doubt, that person did their research and *chose you* to work with. Without any special treatment, that humble engineer will tell all of their friends and family how proud they are of the work you did for them, and in consequence, you will have their whole family tree lining up for appointments out the door for the rest of your lifetime. You will build a solid relationship with that engineer and have the privilege of really getting to know who they are, the successes that they've celebrated, as well as learning from any mistakes they've made. That engineer will inevitably become your friend and eventually you will see them as an extended family member. The key words are *value* and *relationship*. These are the two components for the longevity of success. I'd rather have a whole tribe of peers carrying me than any single famous person. The journey to success is a marathon, not a sprint.

On the other hand, it's important to recognize that in most cases, celebrities or influencers who seek your services won't typically share the tattoo on their social media, whether they pay for it or not. You're unlikely to see them again after the initial appointment. They won't show genuine interest in your life or how your business thrives. They came to you for the benefits and because it was convenient, as they happened to be in town. They won't actively encourage others in their circle to seek your services because they don't truly understand or appreciate the value of your work.

The most difficult part for me was finding a balance between being a professional and being a friend, a listening ear. I had this ability to sense and absorb people's emotions. So, when I had clients who were struggling students, grieving, or single parents, I couldn't help but feel their pain. I often charged them very little or nothing at all, taking on their suffering instead. But on the bright side, this vulnerability helped me build strong relationships with these individuals. I think it was a combination of my values and lack of confidence that ultimately contributed to my slow progress towards success.

UNBOUND

I t was the beginning of 2010 when I made the decision to part ways with the shop where I was working. I felt like I had plateaued. My boss was absent most of the time, and I was busting my ass eighteen to twenty hours a day trying to make a mark in the industry. I was so eager to learn more about tattooing and I needed help perfecting the craft but I had no one there to critique me or guide me. The men that I had thought would take me in as one of their own ended up only using me for financial gain. I felt a lot of disappointment during those years, but nevertheless I was still grateful for having been able to get my foot into the door.

My soon-to-be business partner, who had been in charge of my marketing and online presence, proposed that we open our own shop. After a few weeks of hesitation, I decided to take the leap. We didn't know where we would go or how we would go about it, but we agreed to take on the obstacles together as we encountered them. He had some experience in business and he was older than me so he had some credit history, whereas I had the operational experience to be able to get things set up.

On a random midnight, we had a friend come with her truck and like ninjas, we hauled all of my belongings from the studio away. I hadn't realized how much of the studio was decorated with my belongings and equipment. Only when I looked at it for one last time did I grasp how empty it would be without my spirit there. I had poured my heart into this place that wasn't mine for two years with nothing to show for it; no progress. This was a moment of clarity.

This is when I came to the realization of my dedication to others and how I held up that standard more than I looked out for myself. I always seemed to put others' needs on a pedestal above my own. This is not a positive quality in regards to self-love, but it was definitely a quality that inevitably helped my relationship with my clients. My loyalty definitely worked against me in this particular scenario, but I did not let an isolated life circumstance dictate the way I would view people nor would I let it affect the way I carried myself for the rest of my life. However, I was undoubtedly more shielded. It was at this point that I would stop accepting favors and help from people, because my mentality would have to pay it back with a life's worth of debt.

A NEW FRONTIER

My new business partner and I met up almost every day for about six months. We would meet at boba shops or cigar lounges and brainstorm.The routine consisted of picking a retail location available that we saw online, driving there, then scouting out every possible location within four blocks from there. The goal was to secure a location on Convoy Street, where I had been raised. There were no tattoo businesses that existed there yet so I had the intention of establishing the only one, thinking that I had the upper hand. I had been hopeful that this neighborhood would offer me the best chances of acceptance, naive enough to think that fellow Asian business owners would be proud to take in a young Asian entrepreneur looking to bring something new to the table. I was wrong.

The initial phone calls always went smoothly. But once the management company representatives showed up, the tone always changed. We were met with criticism and disdain. We kept getting excuses like "it's no longer available" or "the owner isn't sure you'd fit into the plaza". We received outrageous contract proposals upwards of about ten years, which isn't feasible for a new business. We had no choice but to look to other areas to build our business.

El Cajon Boulevard was a street in East San Diego which was home to over twenty tattoo shops at the time. This was not an ideal place to get our footing because of the given competition,but it would be the *easiest* place to lock in. It was home to many low-income families, but on the other end it neighbored San Diego State University and its students. It was a melting pot–home to hole-in-the-wall restaurants, wholesale markets, insurance agencies, old school barbershops and anything else that you can think of. This neighborhood was where I got in trouble for most of my teenage years and I had many friends there, but it wasn't a place that I wanted to stake my career on. I knew that my business wouldn't be able to grow as quickly as I wanted to. But it seemed like we had no choice.

We soon found a plaza that would take us. But of course, nothing easy comes without its fair share of downfalls. It was an old three-story building built to look like Chinese architecture, run by an Italian-American military veteran and his Chinese wife. There were businesses that existed on the first and second floor, and the third floor contained a few residential apartments (I know it's weird). The parking spaces were only big enough to fit the most compact cars, and you'd need luck to maneuver the two way drive parking lot which was only big enough to be a one way. Behind the building were old apartments and houses resided by holistic doctors, Asian families, drug dealers, and hipsters.

The suite that we had secured was supposedly a thousand square feet, but the owner had failed to mention the detail about how about one hundred of that square footage was a long, awkward hallway from the front door to the rest of the suite. We had no use for this space nor could we do anything with it but put some extremely narrow couches and chairs, and doing so would block the walkway. But we were desperate and overlooked this along with the random office that was built in the middle of the suite, in which the restroom was located (the bathroom had plumbing to contain a shower if we needed it, by the way). The concrete foundation in the suite itself was peeling from the floors and the walls were all crooked. But "beggars can't be choosers," so we seemed to have no choice but to lock this in so that we could get down to business.

At the time, there were only a handful of professional Asian tattoo artists that existed in San Diego. I was one of three Vietnamese tattoo artists that existed at the time. Disadvantageous to me, the other two men had been tattooing for over fifteen years and were a staple in their communities in City Heights. One of them, a man by the name of Dang, actually offered me a job when I was only seventeen years old. I used to frequent his shop a lot with the friends that I had hung out with and he had taken a liking to my interest and my developing tattoo skills. However, I had rejected this offer because I wanted to take a different approach and not continue the existing trend and give myself the limitations of comfort. The other artist's name was Hung (Dang used to work at his shop). He was an old school freehand tattoo artist best known for his dragons. If you received an Asian tattoo in the early 2000s, odds are that you got tattooed by this man.

I was a young, hungry artist seeking to make his mark in the city. I defied a lot of the "rules" and "etiquette" when it came to the business. For instance, my business partner was white. I didn't just specialize in Asian tattooing; I took on everything that came my way. There are many artists out there that are financially struggling because they have too much ego and pride. I personally know struggling artists that will refuse work just because it isn't their "style." The only thing I have to say to that is "beggars can't be choosers." You cannot "specialize" in something until you have mastered everything else. Nobody is "too good" to refuse a chance to practice their craft, especially at the beginning of their careers.

Vice versa, there are also many artists who sell themselves out for monetary gain. Some will do every tattoo that walks in even if it defeats their moral values, harms the client's futures, or offends others. Other artists may reach a certain level in their career where they are quick to shut out those who helped them get their start. This is the perfect "career-ending" recipe. As most of these artists' work plateau, they start to care less and less about the significance of each piece and more about how much they can make in the least possible amount of time. This is shameful. When I began my journey as a tattoo artist, I had no choice but to adjust my "style" to "whatever the client wants." This has allowed me to attract thousands of clients; however, it also definitely slowed down my rise to perfection. When you are trying to focus on a little bit of everything, you will undoubtedly be slower than others who start off with a "specialty" from the start of their careers. The true reward, though, is not being bored and not plateauing. I truly enjoy the randomness of the work that I am presented with and I am grateful to have reached a point where I can say that I am proficient in each and every tattoo style you can think of. So I have no regrets in the choices that I made, although it made me a black sheep in the Asian tattoo community.

This new shop of mine inevitably ended up being located RIGHT in between the shops of the other two Vietnamese artists. The tension was unignorable and would play out as the years went by.

JACK OF ALL TRADES

Our initial team consisted of a friend of mine, a tattoo acquaintance I knew, and a friend of my business partner. This team would help lay the foundation of the business and kick us off to the public eye, but in reality they were mostly part-time artists helping out of love. We had non-existent walk-in traffic and most of the days were spent just doing construction and renovations, which we had no prior experience doing. I had to take it upon myself to carry the financial weight of the business with the first month's rent drawing closer and closer all while trying to make it presentable.

It was close to midnight, and I was completely exhausted after working for a grueling sixteen hours straight. However, since only half of the shop had been tiled, we needed all hands on deck for construction. I entered the adjacent suite, which the landlord had been using for storage. That's where we had set up the wet saw. It was my first encounter with any type of saw, so I resorted to watching instructional videos on YouTube and improvising as I went along. As I repetitively followed the motions, up and down, up and down, I found myself slipping into a trance-like state. I glanced at the clock and realized it was almost two a.m.. Suddenly, I looked down and saw that my hand was dangerously close to the spinning saw blade. I was too tired to continue safely, so I decided to call it a night and reluctantly stopped working.

Taking a break during renovations

When you think of becoming a business owner, you often fail to recognize all of the work that falls in the cracks; the fine print. We had to learn how to build walls, how to plumb, how to lay tile, how to paint, how to market, and how to speak with customers on top of keeping those very customers coming back. Keep in mind that I had *NEVER* had a real job other than tattooing, so I knew nothing about customer service besides what I have naturally developed on my own through my few years tattooing at home and the previous two years at a private studio. Lucky for me, I was always good with my hands and tools so I was able to adapt quickly to the "constructive" tasks that I had to deal with, and my OCD deemed advantageous in regards to the aesthetic appeal of the studio.

The dysfunctional foundation of the studio as raw as we inherited it meant that every job that was already difficult became even more difficult. We had no choice but to make do with the scarce budget that we possessed. That meant installing tiles that could literally break with your hands, using the cheapest rubber baseboards that we could find and going with the cheapest furniture we could get our hands on.

A lot of people used to tell me, "Man, you're so lucky you own your own business" or "It must be nice to make your own schedule" or "You make your own rules." The truth is, there were times when I wished I could just work a nine-to-five job without worrying about all of the micro-problems that we faced as business owners. It would have been nice to have people make the tough decisions for me and take the blame when things went wrong. It would have been nice to get raises every year and have set days off every week with hours of paid vacation each year. But I didn't have the luxury of having that option as a result of the decisions I made up to that point in my life. I had to earn the very floor that I stood on. I had to earn the paint on the walls that surrounded me. I had to earn the privilege of walking into that very business that I created.

The first year in business was extremely rough. I was literally at the shop from morning to morning on any given day. I had to tattoo anybody and everybody that would give me the opportunity. I don't know how I did it, but I managed to make just enough for rent each and every month. I was living off of tips, eating chips and jerky for dinner with no other meals in between. My business partner was on the same boat. Each client that didn't show up was detrimental to our survival. But we couldn't show desperation.

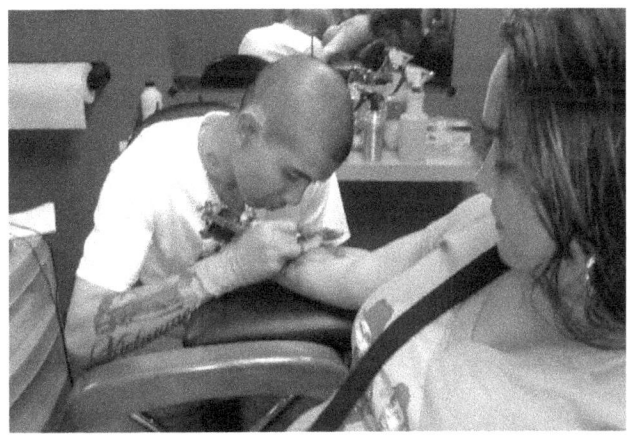

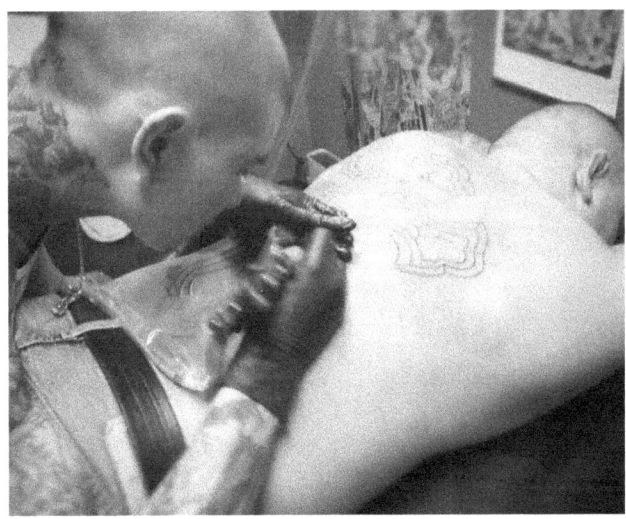

I think that most business owners and entrepreneurs go through the same things that I did, but we tend to forget either unknowingly or purposely. These were dark times but we made the best of it. But the luxury of looking back is only available to those who have succeeded, as I am sure that those who don't succeed live with that failure each and every day. It will eat you up. If I were being honest, I questioned myself about whether I was making the right decision each and every day, but it was too late to turn back. This was my life and I would have to face the inevitable, whether good or bad.

THE TEACHER

At twenty years old, and having been a professional tattoo artist for only two years at the time, I don't believe I had any business teaching anyone anything. I was still a student myself. However, I have always had a talent for uncovering the hidden potential in others, even when they were unaware of their own abilities. Perhaps it was my way of compensating for my own lack of confidence in realizing my own potential.

I had the privilege of mentoring numerous apprentices throughout my career, many of whom were either lacking direction or seeking to break free from the monotonous routine of their lives. What bound us together, without fail, was the shared experience of coming from broken families, much like my own. Within the walls of my shop, a remarkable transformation took place – it became a sanctuary, a place they embraced as their own, and where they wholeheartedly devoted themselves to its protection. The relationships I fostered with each apprentice were truly invaluable to me, and even if some have moved on, I continue to keep a watchful eye on their journeys from a distance.

One of the most rewarding aspects of building my business was the profound connections I forged with both my apprentices and clients. I take great pride in the fact that I not only taught them technical aspects of the craft, but also instilled in them the virtues of hard work and perseverance through my own actions. It wasn't just about imparting knowledge either; it was the multifaceted roles I had to assume for their well-being that proved to be the real challenge. Despite being younger than most of them, I found myself in situations where I had to navigate through their personal issues outside of work, whether it was offering guidance on relationships or dealing with bullies. It required empathy, patience, and a willingness to support them in various facets of their lives. Each apprentice brought a unique set of circumstances, and it was my duty to adapt and provide the guidance they needed.

I taught my apprentices everything I knew, no matter how little that may have been. Watching them grow and escalate and feeding off of their drive and momentum pushed me to be both a better tattoo artist and mentor. Oftentimes I was asked questions that I had no clue how to answer, so I would find out and learn along the way. Teaching others about customer service, financial knowledge, and helping them achieve their artistic goals gave me a deeper understanding of patience and the satisfaction it brings. Assisting apprentices to hone their skills allowed me to revisit the fundamental principles that underpin my own craft. I had to take all the good that I have learned from all of the artists who have come in and out of my life and consolidate them into a master class.

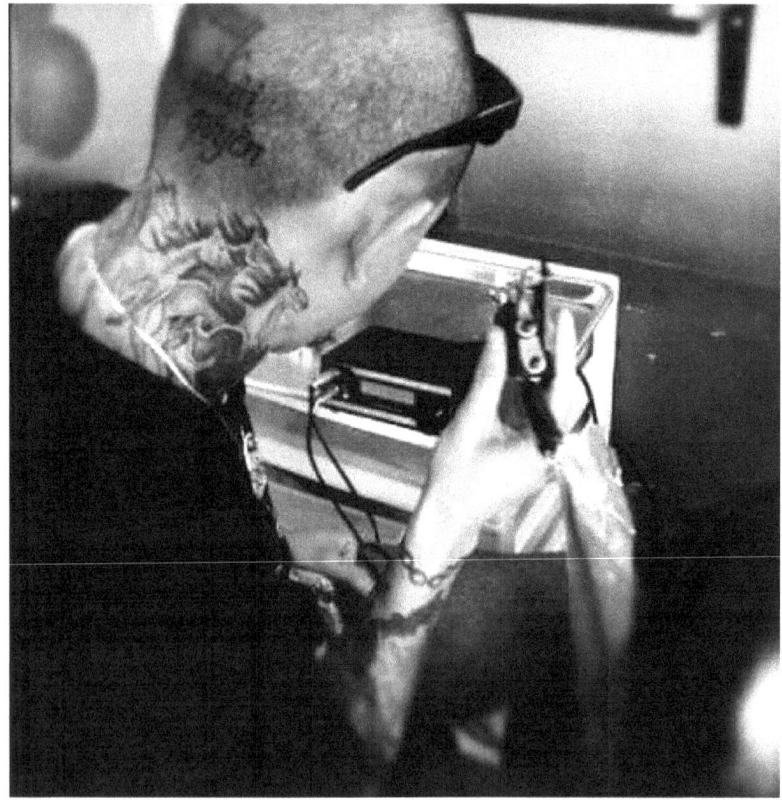

Having a student or an apprentice is similar to raising a child. You are the greatest, almighty, all-knowing individual in their world for a time. They listen to each and every bit of knowledge you have to give until they form their own perspective and construct their own process. And then they reach the stage of resentment, then the stage of thinking they know better than you only to, a few years later, understand the value of what they were taught when they are faced with the challenge of becoming a mentor themselves .

As a teacher, I had to learn how to not compare my disciples to myself–whether it be their upbringing, their interests, their approach, or their drive. The biggest mistake you can make as both a parent and a teacher is expecting those who look up to you to understand you. No two people face the same obstacles. For you to scold another for having different obstacles to overcome is ineffectual and only distances you further from them. People mistakenly teach their disciples to be replicas of them, when they should be highlighting students' distinct individual characteristics. The only common traits between you and your disciple should be the basic roots of your understanding. You cannot control which ways the branches grow. You can only simply watch them grow and trust that you watered the soil.

As a teacher, you cannot expect to feel appreciated or valued. You just have to know in your heart that you are doing all that you can to help another human being and that they won't know any better until your teaching is done. I spent almost all of my downtime during the course of my career making the effort to plan and execute learning experiences such as self-tattooing, mock consultations, and diversifying the artistic repertoire for my apprentices. I sacrificed money I could have made during those hours to build an individual into someone they were proud of. I never once took money from any of my apprentices and always tried my best to take care of them with what I had. As a spectator to my work ethic, adversely, some of them became numb to watching me work for eighteen hours a day. They became numb to the loyal clients who repeatedly showed up each and every month. It got to a point where I feel they lost their appreciation for how amazing it was for an individual to be able to work like clockwork, like a machine.

Regardless, looking back, if there is one thing I can truly be proud of in my life, it is knowing that I played a part in building a brighter future for these remarkable individuals.

Some say that the only way to prevent war is strength. But being a mentor and a boss isn't as simple as black and white. You often question yourself on whether or not it's better to lead with love or to lead with strength. The truth is–damned if you do, damned if you don't. You must work through trial and error to mix a perfect balance of the two in order to reach the peak of respect. Both of these qualities are necessary to deal with the complexities of your position of power effectively.

THE RISE

In 2011, I got extremely sick. Maybe it was, in part, due to the amount of work that I had been trying to kick out in combination with the lack of sleep and clients getting me sick. I was out for almost a month. Within that time period, my appointments stacked up on top of one another. By the time I was ready to come back to work, my schedule was full for the next month. This was the beginning of my rise to becoming a tattoo artist that no one in San Diego could deny. It was like my body and my brain rebooted. My determination and my hustle were in overdrive. Before I knew it, I was beginning to get booked for two months, three months, all the way to a whole year. I cranked out three to five tattoos each and every day, and it was like a buffet of business. I had so many potential clients that I had to learn to delegate them to my other artists. The surge of business pouring in was an absolute dream come true, granting me a long-awaited sense of fulfillment. Along with this newfound success came the daunting task of handling it all.

Throughout my career, I had grown accustomed to battling relentlessly for every ounce of business, investing endless hours in self-pro-motion, pleading for clients, and compromising my pride just to attract a few customers. I was never prepared for the challenge of managing a jam-packed schedule, brimming with countless sessions, and enduring constant late-night phone calls from potential clients. I began to realize that I was falling behind on my drawing assignments, prompting a profound realization that a complete restructuring of my life was necessary to meet the soaring demand. Undoubtedly, it proved to be an overwhelming experience. Yet, with the passage of time, I managed to regain control amidst the chaos. I imposed a strict discipline upon myself, striving to adhere to the best possible schedule, even though it still demanded a commitment of approximately sixteen hours each day.

This was a blessing but also a curse. Most clients were straying away from the other talented artists at my shop, andI became increasingly aware that I was inadvertently enabling this dependency. Delegating tasks and placing trust in others had never been my strong suit. Nonetheless, as a new business owner, I recognized the necessity of mastering this skill. After all, the ultimate aspiration of owning a business is to cultivate a self-sustaining operation that can thrive independently. Ultimately, I made the decision to make myself visibly unavailable, so the only option was to find a private studio for myself.

Private studio

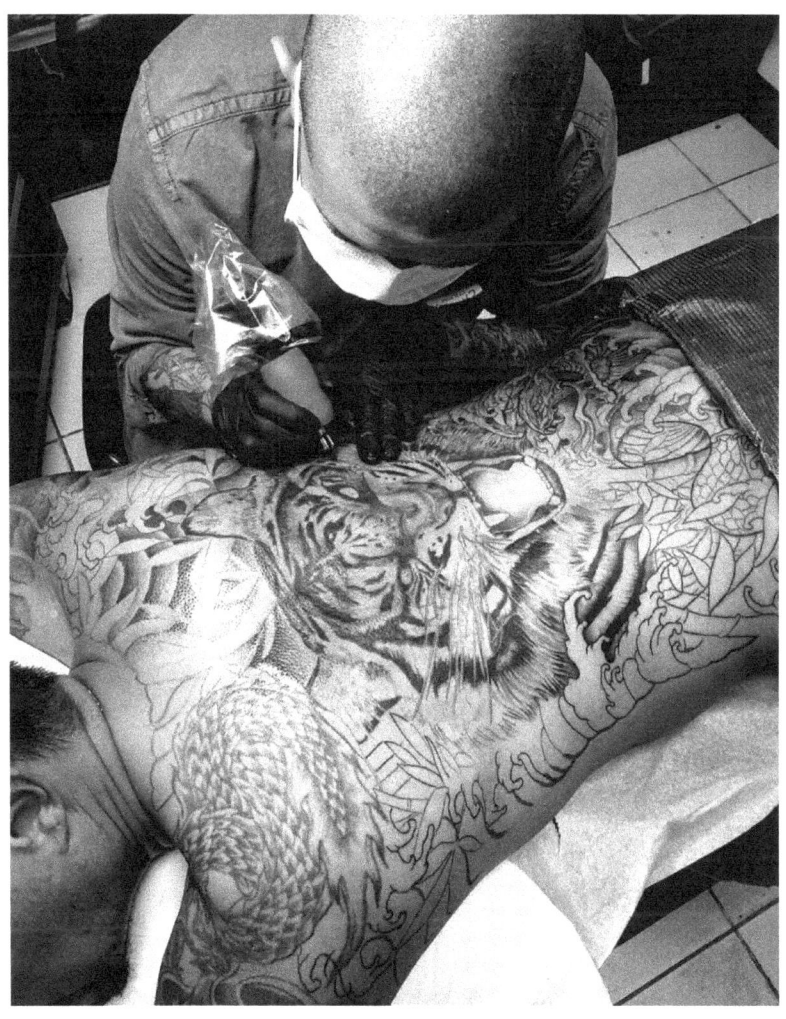

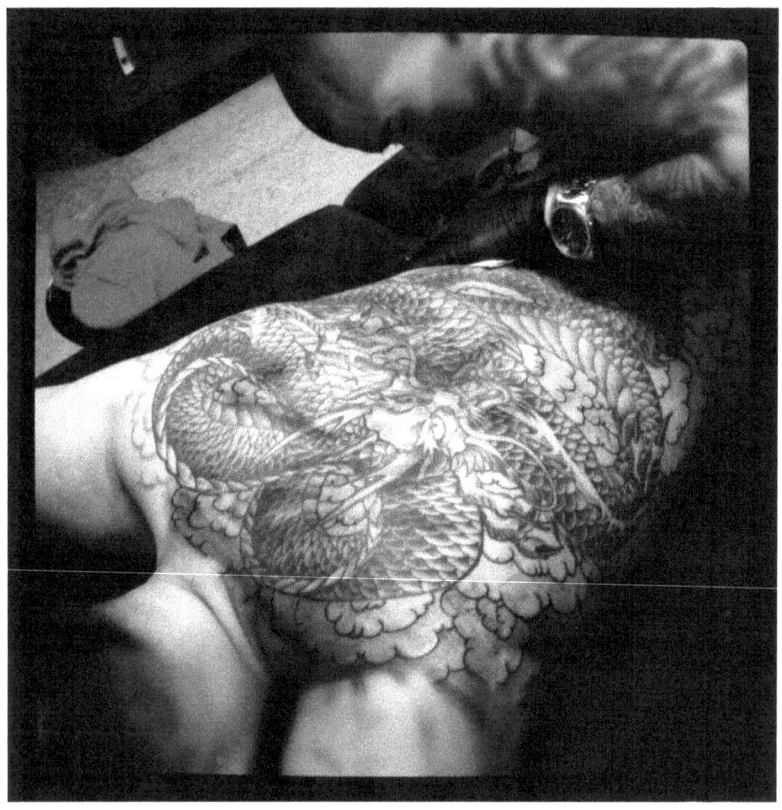

Spending two years alone in that private studio every day forced me to contend with my thoughts and push myself to new heights. Every few months I chose a tattoo artist that I had idolized to study their work, mimic their work, and eventually surpass their work and then move on to the next challenge.

I was not born an artist. Though I had some natural talent, the cultivation of my skills derived from relentless repetition and practice. I ingrained my artistic knowledge into my soul until it was all muscle memory.

My unique tattooing style wasn't something I planned. It came about accidentally as a result of combining different tattoo styles that I knew, specifically realism and Asian work. My technical precision in tattooing, along with this blend of styles, allowed me to create a versatile style that could meet any client's desires.

However, because I didn't have a clear artistic vision from the start, I often felt like an imposter. I never believed my work was good enough, even now. As a result, I undervalued my work and hesitated to charge higher prices because of my insecurities. I used to think that my low prices kept clients coming, but in reality, it was just my lack of confidence. Although this is something I have to carry, it has also pushed me to work harder to keep improving.

During the initial months of my absence, the shop faced its fair share of challenges. Being a place that welcomed aspiring tattoo artists, it often fell upon me to rectify any mistakes they may have made on clients. Balancing the demands of damage control alongside my already hectic schedule proved to be an arduous task, leading to a period of growing pains

The additional burden of damage control brought a sense of chaos and unpredictability to my daily routine. I had to allocate extra time and resources to rectify these mistakes, often rearranging my schedule and squeezing in extra appointments to accommodate the needs of both new and existing clients. Juggling these demands was no small feat, and at times it felt overwhelming.

Amidst the chaos, I remained committed to upholding the shop's standards of excellence. I approached each situation with patience and professionalism, ensuring that both the artists and the clients felt heard and supported. Despite the initial rocky period, we were able to navigate through these challenges and emerge stronger as a team.

Through this experience, I learned valuable lessons in managing and mitigating unforeseen setbacks. It reinforced the importance of fostering a supportive environment for budding artists, providing them with the guidance and resources they needed to develop their skills. Additionally, it highlighted the significance of effective communication and continuous improvement within the shop to minimize the occurrence of such situations in the future. These challenges ultimately became opportunities for growth and learning. By addressing and overcoming these mishaps, we were able to strengthen our shop's reputation and enhance the quality of service we provided to our valued clients.

I was finally able to use half of the money I made to live a life.

HOOD RICH

With my first taste of success came confidence. Overconfidence. It was here that I would learn the hard truth about what a little bit of money does to a person. Growing up in a neighborhood made up of predominantly low-income families, we were never taught anything about finance or how to manage it because we never had the surplus to financially plan. I grew up thinking that living paycheck to paycheck was normal. So I figured that was a fail-safe method since it had been implemented for so many communities in the United States. I spent every dime that I earned because I knew that I could make it back. But I was treading dangerous waters. I was chasing a satisfaction that didn't exist. I was climbing a ladder that had no end. It all starts with "a little more can't hurt," until it does.

Why did I work so hard? It was because I never wanted to be scared to walk into a restaurant and wonder if I could afford it. I didn't want to worry about which shampoo to buy just to save a few pennies. But maybe it was also because I needed something to fully immerse myself in, something that would leave me too exhausted to confront my own reflection. I wanted to feel like I had a clear purpose because, if that purpose was lost, I would have to face my inner struggles head-on.

When you achieve all your material goals and complete your journeys, you'll come to understand that success is not just about what you can show, but also about what you can feel. What's truly fulfilling about success, apart from the power it brings, is the freedom that accompanies it. They say "with great power comes great responsibility" because throughout history, humanity has often had all the advantages and lost them due to greed. You can only keep running past the finish line in one race for so long before ending up back at the starting point.

Growing up in the neighborhood that I did, success to a kid was to have enough meals to eat for a day and to obtain a nice, used car that you could supe up to make it look nicer than it really was. The thought of owning a business, a home, having a garage, and having a backyard never occurred to me, nor did I think it would ever be attainable. Your socio-economic status often puts you in a box. Therefore, my measurement of success was flawed.

My connection with cars throughout my life was deeply significant. They served not only as a means of transportation but also as a gateway to escape and freedom. These vehicles enabled me to break away from the limitations of my childhood, allowing me to explore the world beyond the confines of my surroundings. The open roads were like endless possibilities to me. A journey without a destination became a voyage of self-discovery. I found joy in the journey itself, rather than in reaching a predetermined destination. I gained a broader perspective on the potential of rising to greatness. As a result, my aspirations surpassed the notion of merely outdoing those around me, extending to surpassing even the accomplishments of those beyond my immediate circle. Cars became a powerful symbol of personal growth, inspiration, and a driving force for setting higher goals in my journey through life.

I bought over six cars over the course of the two years that I was at my private studio. These were my trophies, as each one told a story about where my thought process was at those particular milestones. However, when you're in the moment, you fail to realize that trophies are nothing more than pieces of metal whereas the true sentimental value is only known to the owner. I was "hood rich" buying old luxury cars that nobody wanted anymore while still living in an apartment and buying stupid things with my new credit cards. With credit cards, I could take my date anywhere, treat myself to whatever I wanted, and finally get all the tools and equipment I needed. It also gave me the freedom to finance a car on my own without anyone else's approval. It felt disturbingly familiar and natural. Maybe the high was in my genes.

The first car I bought during my "fake it to make it" era was a 1993 Mercedes-Benz SEL Sedan. If you don't know what I'm referring to, just think of every mafia movie you've ever seen. It was black on black sedan, leather interior, with self-closing doors and bulletproof glass. Some referred to it as a "boat" because it was almost as long as one. This car meant so much to me.

This was the first car that I ever bought and fully paid off. I definitely got ripped off but I was so determined to prove to myself that I had gotten somewhere in life that the circumstances didn't matter. I thought that it would magically change my life somehow; but that was a delusion (I eventually bought four more Benzes to see if my perception would change).

Although the vehicle was about twenty years old at that point, just knowing that there was a time where it had an owner that paid over $100K for it gave me a sense of pride. As if somehow having this "thing" would give me some type of satisfaction or closure or sense of accomplishment. The truth was—it was nothing but a rich man's leftovers.

About two years later, I was lucky and stable enough to get a newer, but still used, Mercedes ML350. This SUV marked my transition into adulthood. I no longer needed a flashy car with a loud sound system that attracted attention wherever I went. This vehicle represented a young individual who had managed to escape a difficult neighborhood. I learned to separate my work from my personal identity. I felt like this was a moment where I could finally start my personal journey towards self acceptance and loving the person I had become. For a brief moment in time, I felt like I no longer relied on things like tattoos or extravagant cars to fill voids or boost my confidence.

Though the need to fulfill my materialistic desires took a toll on me, they were the very thing that drove my success. Wanting to attain the things I never had and experience the unfamiliar motivated me to do whatever it took to reach those heights. Even though I may dislike the shallow motivation that fuels the journey, the truth is that it's where everyone naturally begins. It's rare to find someone who pursues their passion solely for the sake of it. Without the means to support your passion, it becomes a dead end.

But while we often search through the aisles, shelves, and online listings of Amazon in pursuit of something more fulfilling, it's crucial to understand that happiness cannot be bought. Material possessions might bring us momentary satisfaction, providing a temporary escape from the emptiness we feel. Relying on these things for long-lasting happiness is fruitless. In fact, they can harm us in the end. Instead of filling the void, they can leave us feeling empty, sad, and even more alone amidst a sea of meaningless objects.

And no matter how many cars I had or how much expensive jewelry I had on, the world saw right through me. The streets were an innate part of who I was. No matter how I dressed or how I carried myself, it's as if people could see into my soul when I walked past them.

I walked into the car dealership by myself for the first time. I was twenty years old and believed that I had everything I needed to make a smooth purchase with no hiccups. I figured that I would just walk in and leave with a brand new vehicle in about two hours and be golden. I had excellent credit, financial proof, and determination. The only thing that I didn't account for was the way that I looked.

As I exited my car, an older man immediately opened the front door of the glass dealership building and started walking toward me. I could tell that he was Jewish from the yarmulke he was sporting. He wore a nice baggy suit, reminiscent of the old days. I put on my best smile and waved at him.

"What can I do for you today?" he asked.

"I'm just looking to browse and narrow down my options. I saw a few used Benzes on your website, and I wanted to see them in person," I replied with confidence.

"Sounds good. Go ahead and take a look around and let me know if you need anything," he said with a nervous tone.

I spotted the used car area and proceeded to walk toward the cars that I was interested in. I couldn't help but notice the man's shadow fixed on mine as if they were traveling in sync. This man was following me as I walked around the whole dealership. Finally, to break the ice, I asked him about SUVs that he had available.

"Sure, take a look at this Escalade that we have; it's probably more in your price range," he said in a smart-ass tone.

Agreeing to play his game, I hopped into the old Escalade and noticed that there was woodgrain trim in the interior of the vehicle.

"Ehh... I don't know. I'm not really a fan of wood grain. I'll probably pass on this one," I said respectfully.

"Oh. Too classy for you, huh?" he snickered.

Annoyed at this point, I proceeded to walk over to an Audi A7 that I saw parked in an isolated area. Before I could even glance at the price tag, I was interrupted.

"Oh. That's a $60,000 car. Way out of your price range. I can't even open it for you unless you're for sure going to buy it."

"Don't worry, I'd never buy an Audi. I'm more of a Mercedes guy. Thank you for your time though. I appreciate it, sir," I said firmly.

"Oh. I worked at Mercedes for twenty-five years. I could get you whatever you want," he snapped back.

"Thanks. I'll let you know," I replied as I walked back toward my car.

For most of my life, I walked into scenarios knowing how my appearance would be absorbed by most of society. But moments that involved large purchases or professional settings always put me on edge. If I got angry, I would be acting exactly the way they had expected. If I didn't react, then I was spoken to like a piece of shit. This predicament caused me to overexert my financial power to impress these people who didn't matter one bit to me. I pretended not to care about interest rates on my cars. I didn't look at the prices on the clothes I bought or looked for sales. Whenever I went to restaurants, I tipped 100%. I did all of these things to make up for what I lacked aesthetically. It was the only thing that commanded respect.

STREET CREDIT

I t was Tết, Vietnamese New Year. My lion dance team already had four performances that day, and we were beat. Being a drummer, my hands were blistering, bubbles of blood waiting to pop. I had them wrapped in tape as I drove four of the kids from our team to the last show at Mira Mesa Recreation Center, where one of our team leaders was hosting the Lunar New Year festival for all of San Diego to enjoy.

Tết, the vibrant Lunar New Year celebration, held a special place in my heart, an annual event I eagerly awaited throughout my life. As Vietnamese and Chinese families rejoiced with their loved ones and paid homage to their ancestors, my lion dance group embarked on a noble mission–spreading blessings and good fortune to homes and businesses for the year ahead. Growing up in a family that didn't extensively observe the holiday, I discovered solace in the profound joy of uplifting others' spirits. Being part of this tradition, I felt a profound sense of pride as I actively contributed to the preservation and continuation of my cherished cultural heritage.

Our performance was the closing show of the night. We were running late because of the traffic, so I found the closest parking spot across the street to avoid circling around the park endlessly.

I parked the car, took off my red beanie, the tape off my hands, and my red shirt to avoid any mischaracterization of being a gang member. I put on a hoodie that covered most of my neck tattoos and made sure the sleeves were long enough to hide my hand tattoos, just to walk across the street for two minutes.

I waited at the stoplight with the kids. "Go ahead and walk in front of me. I'm going to smoke a cigarette," I urged.

I lit up my cigarette and covertly took a drag every ten steps as we walked across. As soon as I stepped foot onto the sidewalk in front of the park, I noticed a police car coming from my northeast side. I kept looking forward and tried my best to blend in with the rest of my team. We were all wearing yellow pants and had our sashes around our waists. NO ONE wears yellow pants unless they're performing or something, right? I guess not.

As the police car passed me, I could feel the officer's neck break as he turned his head towards my direction. I instinctively alerted the kids, "Go ahead and go inside first. We're about to go on stage now. I'm about to get pulled over by this cop right here."

"What? Why? You didn't even do anything," one of them replied, confused.

"Just trust me. You guys go ahead," I repeated.

What seemed like only three seconds after I muttered those words, I heard sirens behind me. There was not just one police car, but two more back-up vehicles to stop little ol' me. They all got out of their patrol cars in unison and rushed toward me, getting in front of my face. The main officer, with his sunglasses still on, was eager to make his authority known.

"Do you have identification? Let me see your identification," he demanded.

One of my teammates in the background shouted, "We're lion dancers. We're about to perform right now. He didn't even do anything!"

The kid immediately ran toward the metal fence where there was already a crowd of Vietnamese people wondering what was going on as the emcee was calling the team to the stage. My friend, the organizer of the whole event, ran toward me.

"What's going on, Officer? He's one of the performers. He's okay," the organizer pleaded.

"Don't worry. We're just checking him out," the officer said with a smile.

I looked at my friend and nodded my head, signaling for him to leave it alone and go inside.

I focused my attention back on the officer, trying to suppress my frustration. "I'm going to reach for my I.D. right now. Is it okay if I put out my cigarette on the floor before I do so? Or would you like me to walk over to the trash bin to toss it before you give me a ticket for littering?" I snapped.

"Haha. Go ahead and put it out right here," he said.

I reached for my wallet, pulled out my identification, and gave it to him. He told me to wait for him to pull up my information, so I sat on the curb for about three minutes as he did what he had to do with his small army. The Vietnamese community inside the festival was still planted in front of the gates, waiting for a conclusion to this chaos. All eyes were on me, so I had to be on my best behavior.

The officer came back fairly quickly. I had a feeling it was because the pressure was on him with all the peering eyes of the whole community on him. He was treading just as softly as I was. As he handed my I.D. back to me, he made a smart remark: "You're good to go. Let the officer up ahead know that I already checked you. Maybe it'll get you some street cred."

I smiled and proceeded to walk in to do my job.

This situation was nothing new to me. I was used to being targeted because of my CHOICE to look the way that I did. That wasn't the thing that was bothering me about the situation. What bothered me was, as a leader to the kids in my group, I did not want them to let scenarios like this feed their yearning to rebel. I didn't want to be the example that made this type of thing seem "cool." It was frustrating. As a veteran who had been in the lion dance industry since the age of four, I tried my best to lead by example whenever I was with them . The focus was on our passion, not on all the noise. We did what we did for the culture and the community.

Shot by Adam Tran

Shot by Adam Tran

Although my relationship with the police today is much more pleasant than when I was a teenager, it took a lot of work through a lot of years to rebuild that bridge. This deep-seated combination of fear and resentment was forged by experience. I've been arrested for wrongdoing, don't get me wrong. But I've also been bullied by law enforcement for doing nothing at all.

This traumatic burden is one that I still carry with me today. I can't drive with my windows down out of fear of getting pulled over because of the way I look, and I can't even walk across the street without being stopped by five cop cars.

It's a complex relationship. I've met many great police officers who have become good clients of mine and I also have a federal officer in my family, ironically.

Although I respect the work that our law enforcement does when it leads to bad people taken off the streets, it's those few bad egg cops that set the tone for my attitude toward them. I've learned to navigate my way through these hostile situations by keeping my mouth shut and just telling them what they want to hear.

I am proud to say that I never allowed these confrontations to discourage my mission to maintain peace in my city. Despite my departure from street life, I remained deeply anchored in my roots. The world knew that and I couldn't deny it. My ascent to the upper echelons of success did not deter me from extending a helping hand to uplift those who shared my journey. Whether it was my friends ensnared within prison's grasp or the emerging troubled youth running the streets, I assumed the mantle of a peacemaker. Through the connection of art, I orchestrated change.

My artistic influence extended across penitentiaries scattered throughout the nation. Meanwhile, my connections with San Diego's gangs furnished me with a unique vantage point—empowering me to interpose between senseless acts of violence and retaliation. My instrument of diplomacy was art—an embodiment of unity and universality.

I had established a unique business that brought together individuals from contrasting backgrounds, the only place where you may witness an ex-convict and a police officer harmoniously sharing a moment as they receive tattoos side by side. In those brief moments, these souls, who might seem worlds apart, could find a genuine connection through their shared passion.

Society often simplifies the essence of art, categorizing it as either beneficial or detrimental, lucrative or insignificant. Yet, art transcends these conventional boundaries, encompassing a depth far beyond the visible surface.

A NEW CHAPTER

After spending two years at that private studio in solitude I began to witness the repercussions of my absence from the larger shop. Initially, when I stepped away, my intention was for them to become more independent and flourish as individual artists. However, it became evident that the general sentiment was that they felt abandoned and left to face failure alone.

It was time for us to take a leap of faith. With nine talented artists all vying for space in our cramped shop, we realized that splitting our forces was the only way forward. And so, I found myself leading half of our staff to establish what is now known as BLVCK LOTVS TATTOO.

We had set our sights once again on Convoy Street, the vibrant Asian District of San Diego. Since our previous attempt to break into this community of businesses, it had only blossomed further. However, months passed without any luck in finding a plaza owner willing to embrace a tattoo business as their neighbor. We were starting to lose hope.

But then, a glimmer of opportunity emerged when we received a call from the management company of Sunrise Plaza. The owner, an older

Korean man with multiple properties, expressed interest in our tattoo business. Intrigued, I met him face to face, unsure of what to expect. It didn't take long for my apprehensions to fade away.

As we toured the two vacant suites that had been unoccupied for four long years, I could sense a change in my perspective. Growing up, I had never been fond of this plaza, finding it lacking in character and vibrancy. Back in the 90s, it had hosted a mix of businesses, from pet stores to dentists and restaurants. But over time, it had transformed into a significant staple in the Convoy community, boasting multiple premier restaurants.

Despite its transformation, I couldn't help but worry about how our neighbors would receive a tattoo parlor amidst their tight-knit community of establishments. Would they embrace us or shun us? It was a lingering fear that haunted me as we considered our options. However, I reminded myself that every beginning comes with its challenges, and we were prepared to prove ourselves worthy of this opportunity.

With determination in our hearts and a shared passion for our craft, we took a leap of faith and decided to make Sunrise Plaza our new home. Little did we know that this decision would mark the beginning of an incredible journey, not just for our tattoo business, but for the entire Convoy community.

Juggling the construction of the new shop while still maintaining my responsibilities at the private studio proved to be an overwhelming endeavor. With about fourteen hours of work each day at the private studio, I had to find the time and energy to drive to the new location and oversee its setup. While the landlord had generously handled the demolition, our financial situation wasn't particularly robust, making it challenging to invest a substantial amount of money into constructing the new shop according to our vision.

Inevitably, I had to make the difficult decision to charge some of the necessary expenses on my credit cards, putting my pristine credit history at risk. Additionally, we had to allocate almost all the funds from our other businesses just to bring the new studio to a point where it would pass inspection. It was a risky move, but we believed in the potential of the new shop and were willing to take the chance.

With limited resources, we had no choice but to take on the buildout ourselves, occasionally receiving assistance from our friends and staff. It was a steep learning curve as we tackled tasks such as tiling, electrical work, plumbing, and constructing walls. Each skill required patience, attention to detail, and a willingness to learn on the fly.

The days were long, and the work was grueling, but we pushed through, fueled by our passion and determination. We learned invaluable skills along the way, honing our abilities and expanding our knowledge base. Each hurdle we cleared brought us one step closer to realizing our dream of a fully functioning and visually appealing studio.

The process of exercising self-reliance and perseverance taught us the true meaning of hard work and dedication. It deepened our appreciation for the effort and craftsmanship that goes into creating a physical space from scratch. We also learned the importance of leaning on our support network, as the occasional help from friends and staff made a significant difference in the progress we were able to achieve.

As the buildout neared completion and the studio began to take shape, a sense of pride washed over us. We had transformed an empty space into a vibrant and inviting environment where creativity and artistry could thrive. The challenges we faced and conquered throughout the construction process became badges of honor, reminding us of our resilience.

BLVCK LOTVS TATTOO

It was the inspection that would determine the fate of our humble shop. Determined to get things done, we decided to pull an all-nighter, giving our blood, sweat, and tears into the finishing touches it desperately needed. Every little detail mattered immensely. We meticulously attended to every aspect, from the seamless closure of restroom doors to adherence to ADA regulations, even down to selecting non-porous baseboards. The gravity of even the slightest oversight was significant–a single mistake could result in paying rent for a non-revenue-generating space, further delaying progress as it would require a second inspection. With bleary eyes and weary bodies, we meticulously cleaned every nook and cranny, ensuring that every surface sparkled with newfound life. We rearranged the shelves, carefully organizing our furniture in an inviting and eye-catching display.

As the first rays of sunlight peeked through the windows, we stepped back to survey our work. The transformation was awe-inspiring. The once lackluster empty space had been reborn into a place of beauty and charm. It now exuded an aura of warmth and possibility, beckoning passersby to venture inside.

Filled with both excitement and anxiousness, we awaited the arrival of the inspector. Time seemed to stretch on forever, our hearts pounding with anticipation. Finally, the moment arrived. The inspector stepped through the door, her eyes scanning the meticulously crafted details of the shop. We passed the inspection effortlessly.

Relief washed over us, mingled with a surge of pride. Our hard work and determination had paid off. The inspector's words of praise were like music to our ears, validating our efforts and igniting a newfound belief in our abilities.

With this small victory, we knew that the journey had only just begun. The shop we had initially settled for, out of practicality, now held the potential to become something truly extraordinary. We set our sights higher, envisioning a space that would not only make us proud but also become a cherished destination for the community. Being the sole tattoo establishment on Convoy Street, we had the unique opportunity to pave the way for the normalization of tattoo shops in the neighborhood. Our presence here marked a significant shift in the perception and acceptance of tattoo establishments within the community. By showcasing our professionalism, artistic talent, and commitment to delivering exceptional service, we were able to gradually break down the barriers and dispel any lingering stigmas associated with tattoos. Since our inception, we have witnessed an exponential growth in the number of tattoo businesses that have sprung up in the area.

This proliferation of tattoo businesses not only reflects the growing acceptance of tattoos as a form of self-expression but also demonstrates the economic viability of the industry. Convoy Street has transformed into a vibrant hub for tattoo enthusiasts and artists alike, attracting a diverse range of talented individuals who contribute to the local art scene.

Looking back on that all-nighter, we realized that it was more than just a moment of triumph. It was the catalyst that ignited a fire within us, propelling us forward on a journey of self-discovery and transformation. And as we stood in the midst of our bustling shop, surrounded by the beauty we had created, we knew that the possibilities were endless and that our dreams were well within reach. We remain grateful for the opportunity to have been pioneers in this movement. It is a testament to the power of passion, creativity, and community in shaping societal norms and embracing the beauty of body art.

ABANDONMENT

It was a typical day like any other. Or so I thought.

I arrived at the shop extremely early, being the first one there as usual. The sun had just risen, marking the beginning of another day. Following my morning ritual, I prepared a cup of sizzling hot coffee and sat down on the lobby couch to review my calendar while mentally preparing for the day ahead. As I took out my phone to confirm my appointments for the day, I was surprised to see a text from my first apprentice, who also served as the head artist at my other shop. The message had been sent at four that morning, prompting me to quickly open it, assuming it was an urgent personal matter that he needed help with. My heart sank as I discovered it was a lengthy farewell message from him. The text message expressed his gratitude for the opportunity to work alongside me and an apology for the need to move on. That surreal moment left me in disbelief, and I initially dismissed it. To verify that it wasn't some sick prank, I hurriedly opened my security camera app on my phone to check the state of my other shop. The tattoo studio appeared empty, depleted of the tattoo machines, toolboxes, and decorations belonging to three of my most experienced tattoo artists, all of whom were once my apprentices. I couldn't comprehend it. I called my business partner, who lived near the shop. He answered with a groggy voice. I hesitantly said to him, "Go check the shop. I think three of our guys left." His sleepy voice quickly transformed into anger as he replied, "What the fuck do you mean? Are you fucking serious? Motherfucker. Fuck. Fuck. Fuck. Fuck. Fuck. Okay, I'm gonna go over there." We immediately organized a meeting with ALL of our staff. Only three artists remained at the other shop, while the remaining four were at the second location that I managed.

We all sat there, overcome by silence and disbelief that three members of our tattoo family had chosen to depart in such an abrupt manner during the early hours of the night. Did things reach such a point that they couldn't even extend us the courtesy of a proper farewell? Despite our disappointment, we had no choice but to gather ourselves and continue moving forward. Over the next few months, we recruited another artist in an attempt to revive the spirit of our old shop.

The three remaining artists established good camaraderie, and we proceeded to renovate the entire shop to meet the specifications of our new head artist. Our new motto simply became "Keep them happy." Financially, things stabilized, and both shops managed reasonably well.

That said, whenever my business encountered significant challenges, I took it upon myself to pick up the pieces. There were instances where we fell short of $1000 needed for rent payment just a day before it was due, forcing me to work sometimes twenty hours straight to rectify such situations. Every time I thought we were finally overcoming the obstacles, new problems arose, causing a constant back-and-forth struggle. Alongside these business challenges, my personal struggles began to take a toll on me, burying me into deep states of depression. I had worked myself numb, becoming a machine with no emotions. Most nights, I found myself reluctant to go home, instead sitting alone in my dim office by myself, with The Weeknd on repeat. I submerged myself in my drawings as I desperately tried to erase the burdens of my predicaments. To find peace, I lit up the coals for the hookah, and drowned my doubts in cognac. I was angry at the world and at myself, as if my more than ten years in the industry had yielded no progress.

The more money I made, the more responsibility I took on and the more people relied on me. I was way out of my depth. I was drowning in debt from opening that place, in addition to managing two car payments and paying rent for my entire family. Trying to find a balance between my personal life and work life became increasingly challenging.

It was during this time that I realized I couldn't effectively juggle being a family man and a hustler. So, I made a necessary choice: I decided to eliminate my personal life entirely, completely revamping myself. It became crucial for me to strive towards becoming the best version of myself. It was the only way that would enable me to offer the best of who I am to others.

For most of my life, I was a chameleon. I was the face that others wanted to see and could positively comprehend. I couldn't show any weakness for fear that it would be used against me. I smiled constantly during my hours of service, but behind closed doors I battled my personal demons. In the solitude of the night, those demons multiplied, forming an army that I had to confront.

After years of torment, in my moments alone, I finally understood that my artistic abilities thrived in the midst of life's darkest moments. It was a dangerous path I was treading. Depression had returned, quietly sneaking up on me once again. Instead of fighting it, I chose to take advantage of it. Every now and then, in the solitude of my office, during those nights filled with mental torment, I would test the limits of my own existence.

When does it get easier? When you *finish*.

I sat there, clutching the hookah pipe in my hand, while my cup of Hennessy on the rocks sat by my side. The drawing in front of me had drained me, leaving me with no distractions from my thoughts. I yearned to just *feel* something, anything. I needed to break myself so that I could get myself together. I cautiously walked over to the safe in the corner of my office, making sure to check the camera to ensure none of my staff were on their way in. I dialed in the code to unlock the safe and reached inside, feeling for the cold Glock 22 resting there, urging me to use it. Slowly, I walked back to my desk and stared at the wall, turning the music up until the walls shook. I pushed off the safety, pulled the trigger back, and pressed the gun against the side of my head with force, leaving a mark on my skin. Tears streamed down my face, down to my neck, forcing me to confront my darkness. Was life so painful that it was time to end it all?

After about five minutes of madness, I put the gun back in the safe. I walked back to my chair and sat down, then unleashed my emotions onto my phone.

"*In life there have been some dark sagas. I was forced to produce my own bright sagas. I was forced to create a vision of idealism, success, unconditional love, and the portrayal of the peak of satisfaction.*

I am in no way oblivious that this creation of a life filled with meticulous, mindful cultivation of every variable was really a mask that I had glued to the face of reality. The reality of a soul so dark wounded by a past so dark that it would frighten even the worst of madmen. I fight with no one but myself in my psyche each and every day. Some days are more difficult than others but I was able to master the art of calmness, the art of control.

But when an event such as recent has occurred, one can no longer contain the darkness from overwhelming one's soul. To be constantly reminded of the failures and the uselessness and the worthlessness of oneself by oneself is a beastly war in itself- but when the oppression comes from those you love- it strikes the core of the human being.

As I walk to a destination unknown, for an amount of time unknown... I find myself walking towards a bridge– then walking back. I find myself jumping in front of the road-only to jump back. I find myself leaving home– but not feeling like I have a home to run back to. I find myself living a life– but finding no purpose in re-engaging with that life any more.

My soul is confused, as is my mind. On how one can punish oneself inflicting deeper wounds than any opposition can ever cultivate. I am my own worst enemy. I fear myself more than any single being.

And now I cry for help."

Notes to Self (2015)

"I have spent my entire life putting others above myself. I have spent my entire life catering to the satisfactions and desires of those I surround myself with. I have spent my entire life loving others more than myself. I have spent it all focusing on the well-being and the conclusion of other's lives—as I had already known the character of my demise which would indeed be inevitable. I have come and I have gone. I have had nothing and I have had everything. It's ironic how life works. One moment you're hopeless, and the next moment you can't be stopped. But it seems like when you hit the peak, the world decides to knock you right back down over the wall. It's strange in that way. I have always either had it all or nothing.

A lot of you know me as a positive, loving, and passionate guy. but it wasn't always that way. I was once a man with a soul so dark that I was even scared of my own self. A darkness that drove my passion to heights you couldn't imagine.

I have come back to that dark place. And there is no one there to save me... and this is the self destruction I have created."

Notes to Self (2016)

These moments of reflection allowed me to metaphorically die while still alive, all so that I could reincarnate myself yet again.

I bathed in the darkness and trained myself to thrive within it. As my mind expanded and my experiences grew, I was able to take myself out of the present and view my life from a third person's perspective.. I had mastered the art of gaining complete control over my own being. This allowed me to detach myself from my own perspective and observe myself and my life from the viewpoint of others.

I found that instead of trying to fight or relegate my past and my shadow, I would have to integrate them. No longer would I push these demons to my subconscious, but I'd go on to learn to awaken these demons to the surface so that I could not only face them, but utilize them advantageously toward my goals. I accepted my past and forgave myself and those I forbid with the realization that one and life could not be perfect. Wholeness is made up of both good and evil as well as the balance of light and darkness.

Although this darkness is an innate part of us, we blind ourselves to its existence because society and family have subconsciously trained us to do so. We were trained at birth to repress that which might bring criticism or punishment. We hide our negative qualities from others and ourselves and deflect from criticizing and condemning others to discharge our own flaws. We must come to realize that everyone carries a heavy burden of imperfection with them, and the longer this burden is contained, the darker and denser it becomes.

We have to understand that repressing our expressions for fear of consequence creates a different consequence. These expressions do not disappear into the abyss, but hide within our subconscious, fighting to seep out of every pore of your existence. You become a victim of possession to your own shadow. Erich Neumann wrote, "Man has to realize that he possess a shadow which is the dark side of his own personality; he is being compelled to recognize his 'inferior function', if only for the reason that he is so often overwhelmed by it, with the result that the light world of his conscious mind and his ethical values succumb to an invasion by the dark side. The whole suffering brought upon man by his experience of the inherent devil in his own nature–the whole immeasurable problem of 'original sin', in fact–threatens to annihilate the individual in a welter of anxiety and feelings of guilt ." You must *become* hell to *overcome* it.

My whole life was dedicated to making other people happy and meeting other people's expectations of me. I had created the very reliance on myself that I dreaded. For all of my life, I had put my own needs and my own dreams second to all. It wasn't that I stopped loving myself–it was that I never even had a chance to feel what self love was like. I had no reference point for any such thing. To my parents, every overachievement wasn't applauded because it was a mandatory expectation. I had conditioned my peers and my romantic partners to expect me to give more and more until I had nothing left to give. I had made my staff immune to relentless hard work as I showed them each and every day to the point that they KNEW they could always depend on me to keep their workplace alive. I had trained my clients to view me as a working machine with no human limits. I had no one to blame but myself. I was trapped in a box of my own making.

It all comes back to the repeated feeling of abandonment in my life. I was afraid of being abandoned by everybody and anybody the way I was abandoned by my own mother and my brother. I fought relentlessly for everyone around me so that I would never endure that excruciating pain ever again.

The human desire to be accepted and loved by others is a given. Yet, to accept and love ourselves is one of the most difficult feats you'll ever face in your life. This self-abuse derives from self-rejection which is fueled by the need to become the *perfect image*–an image that stemmed from familial and societal pressures and expectations.

My purpose wasn't really MY purpose. It was everybody else's purpose that I was trying to fulfill. This realization deciphered my numbness and detachment to the losses of my friends and loved ones around me throughout the years. It seemed to unveil the intricate layers of my psyche and its intricate ways of self-preservation, unraveling a complexity of emotions that had previously remained enigmatic.

One of the rare days I took off of work for Grandma's funeral. My cousins David (left) from Belgium and Aurelien (right) from France

DÉJÀ VU

About a year later, *déjà vu*. I got a phone call from my business partner early in the morning. "They're gone," he said. I had to let it sink in. The new artist that we had brought in had joined forces with our three disciples to venture off on their own and establish their own shop. We had created our own demise. Like we put the movie on replay, we watched the camera footage as the four of them took off in the late hours in the night with all of their belongings, leaving an empty suite that resembled the eeriness it possessed when we first moved in that place in 2010.

Over the next two months we went against our own "in-house only" principles and just started hiring random tattoo artists off of Craigslist. As we were not built to be a walk-in shop, we couldn't get them to stay, nor did it matter because their lack of clientele didn't do us any good either.

Eventually, we decided to sell our first business. Almost like fate, a competing shop nearby was facing eviction due to the reconstruction of the entire plaza by its owner. Just in time, we presented our offer, and they gladly accepted it, considering it a bargain.

My business partner, who had been solely responsible for managing that shop, took the news very harshly. He blamed himself for its downfall even though we both knew it was out of his control, and his life made a complete turnaround. He made the difficult choice to spend the remainder of his days in Southeast Asia, seeking tranquility and inner peace.

It was at *that* point that I had to take all of the dynamics of the business upon myself. But first I had to unfuck all the chaos.

I've always had a saying, "I will never fire you, you can only fire yourself." Over the course of the two years, those who didn't fit the mold inevitably left. I was then able to run my business as a hybrid of being a businessman and an artist myself. It was delicate to navigate, as most artists are indeed very in tune with their emotions. It took me a long time to figure out the correct management approach to keep my artists happy, motivated, and dedicated. My work ethic never changed, and I wanted to be there each and every day to show them the gratification of hard work. I was the first one there each and every day and the last one to leave. I never left anyone behind. I wanted to instill that sense of camaraderie because I didn't want to be surrounded by anyone who expected any less.

As I learned how to take on all aspects of the shop, including both administrative and operative roles, I was able to develop a trust-based system. It awarded consistency and hard work that allowed my artists to grow both in their tattoo careers and in their personal lives. I focused on consistency rather than trying to push financial quotas. I used all of the business finances toward improving the workplace for my artists. It was our second home, so the urgency to make it a place where both they and their clients felt comfortable was of utmost importance.

❖

As my business continued to grow, there were moments in between that seemed uneventful, yet oddly peaceful. It was a time when I didn't have to worry anymore about whether or not the business would still be standing the next day.

The shop thrived as my talented artists stepped up, finally granting me the freedom to focus on re-establishing my personal life. In 2019, I embraced the commitment of marriage, and the following year, we embarked on the exciting adventure of building our very first home. It was a dream come true, having a front yard, backyard, and even a garage–things I never thought possible.

Photo Credit: Jenny Thai

Yet, amidst these personal milestones, the world faced a grave threat that forever altered our lives. Just when things were starting to look up in my life, the universe shut it down.

LOCKDOWN

A s we reached the halfway point on our home build, the world came under siege by an enemy that we couldn't see. We first saw it in China, then Europe. But we never expected it to travel so rapidly into the United States. We had never encountered anything like it–something that the strongest nation on the planet couldn't stop in its tracks. We had no defenses against this invisible enemy. The only strategy was to hide.

As I followed the news, we got word that we had to shut down our business. I couldn't believe it. I thought it was a joke. But they were dead serious. People were dying left and right and hospitals were getting overrun.

It was a grim day as I had to notify my staff that their livelihood was lying in the balance. They would have to file for unemployment. We didn't know when quarantine restrictions would lift or when the mandated business closures would end. I had to cancel a week's worth of clients at a time.

This was the first time in fifteen years that I was faced with not being able to work. I had no backup plan. I had a physical business that couldn't generate any money for who knows how long. I was scared, but I was hopeful.

I tried to apply for grants, assistance, loans, all of the above. But as a "tattoo parlor" my business kept getting overlooked. While billion dollar companies were getting money and my neighbors were receiving assistance, I got nothing. There was nothing else I could do but wait for a miracle.

I was not only dealing with the shutting down of my business. During the peak of the pandemic, we found out that my dad had stage three lung cancer. He had gone to the doctor about some pain on the left side of his ribs. Come to find out, there was nothing wrong with the left side besides muscle pain. It was the right side where doctors discovered two areas of cancerous growth. I had never seen my dad so scared in his life. Over forty years of smoking, and it took this tragedy for him to realize that it was catching up to him. For the first time in his life, he filed for disability with his company. And I would be the one who would have to help him navigate through this new journey to recovery.

It's funny how life works, isn't it? I, being the son that was destined for failure—the screw-up, the black sheep—was the one who would ultimately hold my father up on my shoulders. I took care of his life's expenses, including his cancer treatment, and I checked on him regularly.

Although my dad and I never really saw eye to eye, the truth is that he was still present for me throughout my life. Seeing my dad at one of his lowest points hurt me deeply. I was scared, especially with him going through all this while a virus was running rampant everywhere. I couldn't fully grasp the fact that my dad had grown older. It was a reality check for me, making me truly realize how delicate life is. I had been so focused on seeing him as the person he had always been in the past that I didn't notice how much he had changed.

This situation made me deeply reflect on how our relationship has grown since the fight we had many years ago. Despite the emotional distance between us, I felt that he held onto me as a reminder of the positivity he had left in his life. Dealing with our differences over the years has made me more patient with people in general and has helped me grasp the true beauty of forgiveness. Releasing my anger toward him set my mind and heart free. Finally, I was able to move on and focus on the next challenges in life instead of holding onto a grudge that no longer served any purpose.

HATE IS A VIRUS

As the deadly COVID-19 pandemic unfolded and claimed the lives of millions, including some of my own relatives, it became apparent that accountability was necessary.

We started to experience a surge in anti-Asian hate crimes across the United States and around the world. The culprit for this hate was the rhetoric surrounding the virus, terms such as "Chinese virus" and "Kung Flu" that were used by many political leaders and media outlets. This sparked a dangerous narrative that led to the discrimination, harassment, and acts of violence against the Asian community as a whole. We became targets of verbal and physical assaults, intimidation, and vandalism. The assailants targeted mostly the vulnerable, elderly, and women.

It is important to acknowledge the tremendous diversity within the Asian American community, comprising individuals from different ethnicities, cultures, and nationalities. Despite this diversity, the acts of hatred witnessed during this time indiscriminately targeted anyone perceived as Asian, irrespective of their unique backgrounds. All the progress that we worked so hard to establish in this country seemed to have diminished overnight. While this tragedy alienated Asian Americans from the rest, it brought us together for the first time in a long time, to fight back.

Witnessing this disturbing trend, I felt compelled to take action, but I was unsure about how I would make a difference. For the first time in my life, I was angry and couldn't do anything to help the situation. I had no clue how to help. This wasn't my arena, and I was beyond frustrated. So I did the only thing I knew how to do.

With my business shut down and plenty of free time on my hands, my daily routine consisted mainly of rescheduling my clients. One day, as I scrolled through Instagram, I stumbled upon the nonprofit organization named Hate Is A Virus. They were spreading awareness through various forms of art, which sparked an idea within me.

I sat down, got on Procreate on my iPad, and started to draw. My aim was to capture the struggles faced by AsianAmericans in the United States. To symbolize the current times, I depicted an Asian woman donning a surgical mask. I adorned her with a traditional nón lá (conical rice hat) and Vietnamese áo dài (traditional dress)to represent my cultural heritage. To signify her connection to America, I incorporated the American flag into the sash of her rice hat.

Curious about the response to my concept, I shared a rough sketch on Instagram and it caught some traction. Within twenty-four hours, I had completed a full-color version of my digital painting, "Model Minority," and uploaded it, tagging the "Hate Is A Virus" nonprofit to draw attention to their cause.

I captioned the post with, *"She grasps onto our Nation's flag while her mind is sheltered by her unforgotten culture. She is just as 'American' as the patriot next to her, and she does her part to feed into the system of the country. There is beauty in her diversity, but deep down she knows her acceptance is a gray area."*

The next day when I woke up and checked my phone, I couldn't believe my eyes. The image had been shared by hundreds of people and some news organizations, many messaging me to express how the image captured their emotional torment.

I felt as though I had accomplished my goal. I provided a form of expression for people to share who couldn't otherwise. It was an image that brought people together for a higher purpose. Even though art has captured many pivotal moments in history, I had never imagined that one of my creations would ever be good enough to fall into such a category.

I didn't plan on making money off of my artwork at all. It was created simply for people to share and connect with. I received many requests to turn the artwork into apparel, but having had no experience in the fashion industry, I kept rejecting the idea. I didn't want to make money off of an unfortunate circumstance for our Asian people. It didn't morally sit well with me. Plus, my business was only left standing because I was paying for it solely out of my own pocket. We were bleeding money. I couldn't afford to invest in anything that wasn't a sure thing. Full colored t-shirts cost a fortune to print, and there were no guarantees that anyone would even buy my product.

In the weeks that followed, my wife and one of my closest friends continuously insisted that I print the t-shirts. I kept refusing, but one of my good friends, Lan Dang, who owns several Sharetea franchises in Southern California, put me in a tough spot. Lan had known me my whole life and understood how stubborn I could be. He also knew that I had a hard time accepting help from others because it made me feel like I owed them for the rest of my life. He and my wife undoubtedly believed in me and my abilities more than I believed in myself.

Late one night, I received a message from him: "Send me the file. I've already ordered 1000 shirts. They'll be ready in two weeks."

I couldn't believe it and panicked, "What?! No way, bro. Are you serious? How will I ever sell 1000 shirts?"

He replied, "You'll at least make the money back, even if you don't sell them all. Don't worry."

Exhausted, I pleaded, "Bro, I can't afford that right now. Please cancel the order."

He reassured me, "No need to worry. I'm not in a hurry. You can do it. I believe in you. Do you want all of them to be white?"

Feeling overwhelmed, I hesitantly responded, "Oh my god. Now I have to hurry and create a website and everything, maybe even start taking pre-orders to see what we can handle. And no, let's make half of them white and half black. I'll make a black version by tomorrow."

He agreed, saying, "Okay, I've already ordered 1000 white shirts, but I'll add another 500 black ones."

Shocked, I exclaimed, "Seriously, bro? That's a lot!"

He dismissed my concerns, saying, "Don't worry. Just send me the file."

I was trapped, The only way out was *through*. The next day I started learning everything that I could about e-commerce and its platforms. I started designing the website for BLVCK LOTVS THREADS so that it could later serve as my online store for my shop apparel as well. I was a long-game thinker. Every move I made consisted of multiple moves within it. So if I was going to dive into this world of commerce, I would go all the way. I had to learn about logistics, fulfillment, quality control, and everything else related to selling goods. It was a learning curve since I had never had any job that required me to do any of those things, but it was a fun journey nonetheless.

It wasn't too long before we were ready to start taking pre-orders. And this is when my whole life changed.

I received orders from people all around the world, not just from Asians, but also from individuals of diverse backgrounds, including white, black, Hispanic, and other groups, all showing their incredible support. This overwhelming response was truly amazing. Until that point, my audience had been mainly limited to tattoo enthusiasts, and I struggled to be taken seriously as an artist by other groups of people. With "Model Minority," I managed to attract educators, doctors, lawyers, law enforcement officers, and other community leaders, which proved to be an eye-opening experience for me. I believe that I unintentionally played a part in elevating the perception of my profession and shedding a positive light on it . One of my goals was finally accomplished: helping people see tattoo artists as something other than the taboo they perceived us to be in the past.

Through sweat and tears, my wife and I printed shipping labels, folded, packed and shipped over nine hundred t-shirts as soon as they arrived. It took about three days in total. It gave me a newfound respect for the apparel business and it humbled me tremendously.

From these sales, I was able to keep my business alive until we were finally able to open our doors back up for business seven months into the pandemic. I was able to pay my friend back within a couple months after we launched our sales. I was also able to give a portion of these proceeds to the Hate Is A Virus organization to help them on their mission to aid Asian Americans who had been victimized by both the pandemic and the collateral damage that it inflicted. It felt like a miracle.

The creation that initially began as a random project for a noble cause unexpectedly became the very thing that rescued my business from permanent closure.

ENCORE

When my tattoo studio finally reopened, it was a chaotic situation. I had an overwhelming backlog of around three hundred tattoo sessions to catch up on, leaving me with no choice but to work tirelessly every single day. Postponing any more appointments was out of the question; I simply couldn't afford it. Despite the ongoing spread of the virus, clients sporadically canceled due to contracting COVID-19 . Fortunately, the new safety measures implemented didn't differ significantly from the precautions I already had in place as a tattoo business, with the exception of mandatory masking around the clock.

Not only were we trying to catch up on the backlog, but we also faced the daunting task of dealing with deferred rent for the business and a significant surge in the prices of tattoo and safety supplies. The cost of a case of gloves skyrocketed from its original price of one hundred dollars to three hundred dollars, and each of us went through a box every two or three days. Acquiring masks and essential cleaning supplies to sanitize our work areas became a challenge in and of itself. It was a grim period, and I witnessed numerous tattoo businesses shutting down because they couldn't keep up with the demands of this new normal. Although we were back in business, I was still afraid that I would face the same demise. The apparel sales had slowed down, so I had no more lifeline.

But as always I, as a leader, couldn't let my fear or fatigue show. I carried on and put everything else on the backburner until I finally caught up. In the midst of it, I kept applying for grants and loans. I applied for so many small Asian-owned business grants but it seemed to be getting nowhere. I was on my own.

I arrived at work that day, tired from drawing late and coming in early. I was sipping on my new usual from Starbucks. Triple espresso with three pumps of white mocha over ice in a venti cup with whipped cream on the bottom. I had a moment to sit down before my client arrived so I decided to check my phone for inquiries. I noticed some notifications from Shopify, my ecommerce store platform, which I hadn't seen in a while. I had a surprising fifty purchases out of the blue. I was curious about what was going on so I instantly checked my social media.

To my surprise, my digital painting had gone viral once again. But this time, it was ten fold. This was almost exactly a year since the initial beginning of the amplified attacks on Asian Americans the year prior. And we were starting to see a significant increase in violence against Asian American elders around the United States. It had gotten out of hand. So once again, the internet responded.

My work of art was inevitably shared on the social media of celebrities, athletes, and media companies as well as individuals. I even received requests from Facebook and Instagram to spotlight my artwork for their platforms as well as several news outlets, both American and Vietnamese. There were dozens of rallies around the United States that used my artwork for their signs, posters, and flyers. Activist groups and nonprofits across the world were using the image to get their points across. "Model Minority" was featured in magazines and I was asked by a faculty member of Temple University to display it in the Development and Alumni Relations building. It was unreal.

I went on to do several interviews, including one of the largest Vietnamese news networks in the United States. Who would have thought that a random, Vietnamese American tattoo artist from the hood would ever get a chance to speak to the world and have them listen? I didn't.

Rally in Orange County, California

The San Diego Union-Tribune

Celebrating 150 Years
$4/4 months

PUBLIC SAFETY

For San Diego's Asian community, Georgia shootings compound a year of pandemic hate

SWIPE UP

Lauren Garces is an events and outreach coordinator for the Asian Business Association and a member of the San Diego Asian Pacific Islander Coalition, which formed last year to speak out about hate. (K.C. Alfred/The San Diego Union-Tribune)

Dozens of incidents involving anti-Asian hate have been reported in San Diego County

By KRISTINA DAVIS

MARCH 18, 2021 5:53 PM PT

Courtesy: San Diego Union Tribune

Đằng-Giao/Người Việt

IRVINE, California (NV) – Một nhóm thanh niên gốc Việt tổ chức buổi đi bộ "Walk to End Hate" ở Orange County Great Park, Irvine, lúc trưa Thứ Bảy, 20 Tháng Ba, để phản đối những hành động kỳ thị dẫn đến bạo hành đối với người Mỹ gốc Á và Thái Bình Dương (AAPI).

"Walk to End Hate" là chủ đề cuộc đi bộ của một nhóm thanh niên gốc Việt ở Orange County Great Park, Irvine, vào trưa Thứ Bảy, 20 Tháng Ba. (Hình: Đằng-Giao/Người Việt)

Cô Vivian Lê, trưởng nhóm, cho biết hai vụ bạo hành ngược đãi người gốc Á tại Atlanta, Georgia, và San Francisco, California, chỉ là kết

Courtesy: Nguoi Viet News

'Micro' Aggressions, Large Lasting Effects

A Vietnamese-American woman wears a Vietnamese non la hat and a face mask that says, "Hate is a virus." | Art by Dennis Dizzy Doan

Courtesy: PBS

I eventually ordered another 1000 t-shirts and hoodies to keep up with the demand. But with this new demand and a new set of responsibilities as a voice for Asian Americans around the United States, I started to encounter peculiar issues that I never imagined.

Having thought ahead, I started the process of copyrighting my original painting the moment I started selling apparel the previous year. Copyrighting proved to be a good investment because, before I knew it, people and businesses all over the United States tried to steal , replicate, and sell the image with no other intentions but to profit. As my network grew, the sightings grew. With the increasing popularity of my painting also came more organizations requesting my help although I had already pledged a portion of the proceeds of this particular artwork to Hate Is A Virus exclusively.

I was approached by an organization in late 2021 requesting that I send them the original file of my image so that they could print out the shirts themselves.

"Hey, there. Thank you for the recognition. Unfortunately, the image is copyrighted and I already have an obligation to donate a portion of the proceeds to Hate Is A Virus. Seeing as to how both of your organizations are working toward the same goal, I don't think it would be fair for me to give you the permission to produce the product and take away from that. I'm sorry. I'd be more than willing to give you guys the t-shirts at cost though, or make a monetary donation personally to your cause."

I proceeded to go on their website and donate five hundred dollars to their organization. I never heard from him again.

It was at this moment when I started to see the bigger picture. Although I'm sure there were many organizations that started off with the right intentions and were striving to make the world a better place, there were others that did their work with an ulterior motive. There were organizations *utilizing* this traumatic period for Asian Americans to achieve their other goals, make a profit, and ultimately stray away from their purpose as a whole. I witnessed organizations that started off as transparent, clearly upstanding movements only to become nothing but ranting shells. I started to question myself on where these donors' money was going, who it was going to, and to what cause. And I didn't like it one bit.

FOUNDATION

As a way for me to know for sure that my contributions were going to the purposes that they were intended for, I took matters into my own hands.

On a random night in the summer of 2022, I was lying in bed and decided to propose an idea to my wife.

"Babe, I think I want to start a nonprofit."

"Okay. Do it," she replied instantly.

"Really? I don't know. I was thinking you'd talk me out of it or something. I have no experience in the nonprofit sector. I don't know if I'll be biting off more than I can chew."

"It's a better purpose than all your other crazy business ideas."

"I can't tattoo forever. I want to do something that matters when I retire, and I want to create something that pays tribute to my family who sacrificed everything to get us here. I want us, as AsianAmericans, to be taken seriously and for the world to know that we can play a part in making it a better place. People think you gotta be rich like Bill Gates to make a difference, but I want to show them differently. My family came here with nothing and never dared to dream big; they just wanted to get by. I want to show the world how a first-generation Asian kid in America can give back despite his upbringing."

The following morning, I submitted the paperwork for Doan Incorporated, otherwise known as The Doan Foundation. The Doan Foundation is a charitable organization–a foundation that provides children with the guidance and the resources they need to navigate the world of the arts. The original objective was simply to establish scholarships for teenagers from marginalized communities in Southern California to pursue so that they embark on their careers in the arts, which. As I've previously mentioned, careers in the arts have always been looked down upon in minoritized communities because of their disassociation with "wealth." However, I am a testament to the potential that the arts can have on a kid with no hope. I felt as though society stays so focused on trying to solve so many overwhelming tragedies such as world hunger that sometimes it's the kids in our backyard that are left forgotten. This is why I chose to only focus on Southern California for the time being so that I can try to help the lives of the next generation around me.

I spent all of the time during the processing of the paperwork to learn everything that I could about the nonprofit sector and made the effort to connect with individuals that I could potentially learn from if I encountered any obstacles that I couldn't figure out myself.

I reached out to other organizations that had a good track record within the community and took note of everything that they did right so that I could adopt it into the way that I ran my organization. It didn't matter whether it was a Hispanic, Black, Asian, or White charity, I wanted to run things RIGHT. I wanted to provide the best of everything for the kids who grew up with nothing.

All of my years as an adolescent were spent *wanting*. Growing up in a marginalized neighborhood suppresses your dreams. You grow up with thoughts in the back of your head that constantly tell you that there is a wall that you can't climb. So when I was able to get to the other side of the wall I feared one day going back. I sacrificed all of my life to protect and secure this career that I had somehow magically made a success out of.But once you obtain all your *wants* you start to think about your *purpose*. I love changing people's lives through my art, but I wanted a different approach that would allow me to reach and help more people with the assistance that I wish was available to me when I was growing up

My family came over to America with next to no money, no home of their own for years, no English, no jobs, and no dreams for themselves. They simply wanted a better life for their kids. My father once said to me, "I'm glad you're successful and you can take care of your own. I wish I had something to leave back for you and your brother. I have nothing to give you when I die." I wanted to show all the other minorities like me that a family not made of money–a family that came from nothing–can rise up to the occasion when the world is in need. You don't have to be rich to start giving back, and you don't need to have political influence or popularity to simply lend a helping hand. I wanted this massive undertaking to leave a mark in the world, however small it may be.

My experience with the non-profit sector has been somewhat ironic. But you can draw parallels between it and the tattoo world in certain ways. When meeting new people, it's not uncommon to hear them express surprise, saying, "Wow, I thought you would be so different. You're actually really nice." This subtle comment often implies that they had preconceived negative judgments about you. It's essential to remember that their opinions are based on limited information and their own biases. Stay true to yourself, and let your genuine nature shine through.

Attending my first charity gala as a "philanthropist" was an interesting experience. I was donating a piece of my artwork so I was invited to attend a charity event. I wore a turtleneck sweater under my black suit that night mostly to avoid any awkward stares towards my neck tattoos. As my wife and I sat down, I could sense that we had disrupted a conversation at the table of ten as the rest of the eight guests suddenly went mute. I just smiled, not sure whether to introduce myself or say hello. But as they nervously stared down at the table and their phones, it was clear that they wanted nothing to do with me. As the night went on, I overheard the guests at my table speaking to each other about how they were attorneys and doctors (when they weren't whispering things to each other), and I just continued to talk to my wife about the things that we were observing around us—how things were set up, presentation, the entertainment, the timeline of the event. We were there to learn. As soon as the auction ended, I was introduced to the audience as the artist behind the auctioned painting. Long story short, my painting auctioned off for thousands of dollars. As soon as I walked back to my table of mutes, suddenly they knew who I was.

"Can I get a picture with you?" one of them asked hesitantly as he reached over to put his hand on my shoulder for the selfie.

"Oh, man. I didn't know you were the artist. It's so nice to meet you!" another guest said as his wife nodded in approval.

I didn't let these brief instances of arrogance dictate the way I approached other events. This was nothing new. It wasn't enough to deter my ambition to do good. As the months went by, I continued to put myself in situations where I caused rooms to go silent. I knew that the image of this man, myself, would be engraved into the minds of those who spent most of their lives going places where people who looked like me didn't exist. I was–and am–on a mission to change the world's perceptions. My role as the outcast helped my cause.

A few of our scholarship recipients from our first year as an organization

My first speech at The Doan Foundation Gala Fundraiser

The Doan Foundation's beloved donors, supporters, and friends enjoying Gala night

With my new philanthropic identity, I found myself at an impasse, torn between two perspectives. Having once been in the vulnerable position of the very children I aimed to help, I hesitated to showcase my altruistic endeavors to the world. I didn't seek recognition for the good I did in my community nor did I want the spotlight; I simply believed it was the right thing to do. However, my perception shifted after a heartfelt conversation with the dedicated volunteers at the Ronald McDonald House Charities of San Diego, following my toy drive during the holiday season.

When I arrived that morning, carrying three large boxes filled with toys and books for the children, I was warmly greeted by three compassionate women at the front desk. Their reception lacked any caution or apprehension; they treated me with dignity, seeing beyond the tattoos that adorned my body. They wore genuine smiles. This was heartening.

Upon completing the donor paperwork, one of the women inquired, "Where would you like to have the photo taken, Dennis?"

Confused, I responded, "What photo?"

"The one for our social media, of course!"

Hesitantly, I replied, "Hmm... I'm not sure if I need that. I don't need any credit or recognition. Exploiting those in need doesn't sit right with me."

"You have to do it," she insisted. "It's the only way to inspire others to follow in your footsteps. It opens doors for more acts of kindness. By sharing this moment, you'll be helping even more people, rather than exploiting them. It's essential for promoting our new nonprofit."

Reluctantly, I walked over to the three gift-wrapped boxes, attempting to summon a genuine smile.

SAY NOTHING, DO NOTHING, BE NOTHING

Elbert Hubbard once wrote, "To avoid criticism: say nothing, do nothing and be nothing." These words hold true even today, reminding us that taking risks and pursuing our goals often invites criticism from others because it doesn't meet the "normal" standards. When discussing domestication, we often limit the concept to animals, neglecting the fact that humans too bear the weight of domestication from the moment we are born. Initially, we emerge from the womb in a state of pure freedom. As time passes, society and even the individuals surrounding us shape us to mirror their own ideals or the expectations they have for us, rather than allowing us to become the individuals we sense we are meant to be. This process leads to confusion as we transition into adulthood, resulting in years wasted by pursuing the dreams of others, assuming their identities, and ultimately regretting our own existence.

Every decision in my life that ended up blossoming into success started off with somebody else telling me that I was crazy. While the lack of external motivation can be disheartening, it highlights the significance of inner motivation. If you keep waiting to get motivated, you'll be waiting forever. It is common to hear people talk about their aspirations and plans, yet few actually take action. The wheel of progress can only spin when you work up the courage for that initial push. That's what matters. Embrace failure. Do not be afraid. Success is not magic. There is no secret or equation. It is simply the accumulation of so many failed attempts that you become immune to defeat. Success is a gamble and there's no one more qualified to bet on you besides yourself. If you can't see your own potential and awaken it, what makes you think that someone else can force you to? Failing is an opportunity for learning and growth. The principles of business and life are interconnected in this regard—mistakes are paid for, small victories are savored, and new adventures await.

The words of doubt that linger in your mind have no purpose. They only exist because you allow them to. DO NOT wish for the ability to escape; rather, wish for the strength to push through. Words are powerful. Bruce Lee once said, "Never talk badly about yourself, not even as a joke. Your body doesn't know the difference. Words have energy and can affect you, that's why they're called 'SPELLINGS.' Change how you talk about yourself, and you can change your life." Do not poison your mind with words that don't serve you. Stop letting these words cause you to worry about failures that haven't even happened yet or may not ever. These hypothetical, apocalyptic scenarios only exist because you created them. You have the power to UNCREATE them. We should not allow society to distort our perception of our own worth and sovereignty. We hold the power to shape our own lives.

Resisting self-criticism becomes challenging amidst the constant stream of individuals accomplishing remarkable feats that flood your phone screen. The mind tends to perceive these achievements without considering the underlying journey. It's essential to bear in mind that these triumphs were the product of gradual efforts. Even for the fortunate influencers who stumbled upon sudden fame, they must now commit to a lifetime of sustaining that status.

Our duty is to strive for our best and acknowledge when we have given it our all. Self-criticism should be tempered with self-compassion. Each day brings a different version of our best, but as long as we genuinely exert ourselves, our lives will be fulfilling. Only by recognizing that we did NOT do everything within our power to make the most of each day will our minds whisper words of failure. Life is a pursuit of perfection, not an attainment of it. Be comfortable with the uncomfortable. Avoid jeopardizing your future tranquility merely because the familiar disorder feels comforting.

Live without expectation. Expectation is your enemy. Additionally, be prepared to take losses time and time again. If you are not prepared to lose, then you're never going to win because you're constantly playing it safe. Do not walk the streets of life expecting all of the sidewalks to be perfectly paved or you will face the hardened truth of pot holes in your journey. Expect the worst and hope for the best. We're people, and sometimes we lose. What matters is how many times we get back up. Live with intention and sincerity. Many people only take action when they know they will be awarded for their efforts. These people lack discipline and the authenticity to see that the real reward is the journey in itself and the lessons that they bring. They do the bare minimum because they subconsciously know that they only deserve that bare minimum. The option to be mediocre is a *privilege* that most of us weren't born with. We have no choice but to be anything *but* that.

To truly thrive, it's essential to cultivate a relentless perspective centered on greatness. This entails firmly embracing the belief that mediocrity is never an option worth entertaining. By distinctly delineating your financial circumstances from your internal moral compass, you exhibit a commitment to upholding your integrity and principles. This clarity extends to distinguishing between mere success and genuine greatness, as well as understanding that prosperity goes hand in hand with a spirit of compassion. Embrace the profound truth that the art of living is intricately intertwined with the act of giving.

You won't find my peace by following what's popular or doing what everyone thinks is right. You'll actually feel more peaceful when you're doing things your own way, even if it's not what everyone else is doing. And that new thing you're trying may not necessarily have specific goals or measurable targets. Never settle.

I've certainly made my fair share of mistakes, much like anyone else. What truly matters, however, is how we derive meaning from these mistakes. Learning from them doesn't always happen on the first, second, or even third attempt. The real value lies in internalizing the insights these vulnerable moments offer. I've never claimed to be perfect, and that remains true today. Yet, I'm dedicated to the pursuit of self-improvement with each passing day.

The essence of balance is key. It's in the existence of negatives that positives find their significance. The universe elegantly illustrates this equilibrium as the sun sets and the moon takes its place. Thus, we must embrace both the stormiest of seasons *and* the most serene periods. I've encountered losses on par with my gains, and my capacity for love has been matched by my experiences of hatred. A contented life materializes when we grasp that the quest for perfection only holds meaning in relation to our contrasting experiences.

Most importantly, *be you*. The whole you. Remember that pressure creates diamonds.

www.ingramcontent.com/pod-product-compliance
Lightning Source LLC
Chambersburg PA
CBHW051610120626
46551CB00014B/1743